Bless Your Heart

Susan Green Jaillet

BLESS YOUR HEART

A collection of
short stories
and poetry

Susan Jaillet

by Susan Green Jaillet

DEDICATION

To my wonderful writer's group, Writers One Flight Up—Rod Billette, Jeanne Fluegge, Richard Henderson, April Johnson, Linda Kraus, Mike Miller, Jody Rehman, and Nancy Riikonen—who have encouraged and supported me through the long, sometimes painful, often funny, always fascinating process of writing. We are good friends and loyal partners in crime. Thanks to Richard Huss, editor of Pulse the Magazine, for my first writing assignment. Thanks to Janet Manchon for expert proofreading.

To my brother and sister-in-law, Sam and Ellen Green, and my talented niece and nephew, Robin Mathias and Adam Mathias.

To Doug Parker, my life partner and best friend.

.

If life is just a highway, then the soul is just a car. And objects in the rear view mirror may appear closer than they are.

Jim Steinman

CONTENTS

SECRETS

I am a closet.

My secrets are spilling out

like shoes all over the floor.

MOTHER VIVIAN AND MR. W

Sweat beads her upper lip. Her face is pale as the white classroom walls. Nine-year old Rebecca stands at the second story window overlooking the empty playground, her left hand tight around the grey Boston pencil sharpener anchored in the wooden window frame. Mr. Witherspoon has not returned from the office even though the clock behind his desk reads 4:07 and the classroom is empty except for Rebecca and seventy or so yellow No. 2 pencils, blunt and dull in the box. Exactly eighteen stick up sharp and pointed in the cup.

Eighteen are all she needs. She worries. *Should I do another, just in case? What if he asks me, did you do another one, just in case? Just in case you break one on the way back to your desk? Just in case you trip and one jumps out of the cup, leaps into your eye leaving you blind for life? Just in case someone extra shows up and eighteen isn't enough?*

Rebecca's stomach growls, a familiar sensation. Mother Vivian gives her pearl tea and a vanilla wafer every morning before sending her off to school. A dollop of milk in a cup of hot water and one vanilla wafer.

Rebecca wipes her upper lip with the back of her hand. *Is eighteen enough? Will he want another one sharpened? What will happen if I sharpen them all, fill the box with the pointed pencils, put the lid back on and return the pencil cup empty?* Will Mr. Witherspoon see the humor or will he send her to the office like he did last week after she straightened his whole box of paper clips rather than cleaning the white board as he told her?

Mr. Witherspoon is Rebecca's ride to school, an arrangement made by Mother Vivian over a late afternoon cocktail. Mother Vivian, as Rebecca is told to call her, not mom or mother or even mommy, and Mr. W, as Rebecca is instructed to call him off the school property, spend every school day afternoon having cocktails. Rebecca's job is to make the sandwiches they share as part of the nightly ritual.

"I so enjoy sharing the evening meal with you and Vivian." Mr. W pats her head when he says this. Rebecca places the fluted white paper plate on the coffee table in front of him. A scoop of pale macaroni salad from the store, a plastic fork wrapped in a paper napkin, the sandwich cut diagonally in half like he'd taught her. She fetches an identical meal from the kitchen and places it in front of Mother Vivian. If Mr. W compliments her on being an especially good girl at school, Vivian permits Rebecca to join them at the coffee table. Some days she's even allowed a whole sandwich.

Today only a couple of ounces of vodka remain in yesterday's new liter. A cranberry juice bottle is overturned in the kitchen sink, pink stains mark the dirty white porcelain. "Another dead soldier, Vivian," Mr. W yells into the living room.

"War is hell," Vivian replies, her usual humorless retort to this comment.

Vivian has not moved from the shabby brown sofa during the last half bottle of vodka. "Eat up, Rebecca." Vivian frowns. "Finish your dinner and clean up that mess you left in the kitchen."

"Yes, ma'am," Rebecca keeps her eyes lowered, stuffs the remaining bite of sandwich in her mouth.

"Then do your homework, Rebecca. Clean up your mess, go to your room, shut the door and do your homework." Vivian pats Mr. W's knee. "Bert and I have things to discuss."

Rebecca throws the three paper plates in the trash, wipes the counter clean, then places the empty cranberry juice bottle in the trash. Using a small piece of rusted steel wool she scours the pink stain, leaving a swatch of white in contrast to the dirty stained porcelain. She walks to the living room, sees Mr. W has his hand under Mother Vivian's shirt. A small bit of white macaroni rests at the corner of Mother Vivian's mouth as she waits for Mr. W's kiss.

Mr. W turns suddenly as if he somehow knows she is standing there watching. At school Mr. W can always tell when she returns from a mundane chore he's given her—cleaning the white board, emptying the three-hole paper punch—he can always tell when she returns to the side of his desk to wait for his next instruction, even when he doesn't look up.

His eyes meet hers only for a second before he turns his full attention back to Mother Vivian. Mother Vivian moans and Mr. W pushes her down, lays on top of her.

Rebecca watches Mr. W's ass move up and down, barely visible above the back of the sofa. *Ass*, that's what the boys in fourth grade call the soft bundle of flab that fills Mr. W's pants. "Look at that fat ass," they whisper as he writes assignments across the board first thing each morning. "His ass jiggles like a woman's." The boys are always quick enough to be hunched over

5

their desks, pencils in hand, eyes on their lined notebook paper, before Mr. Witherspoon turns to see who has spoken the taunt.

Rebecca awakens early the next morning and the voices in her head start immediately. *Fat ass, fat ass, Mr. W has a fat ass, fat ass, fat ass, can Mother Vivian breathe when he's laying on top of her like that, if I open my eyes will he be standing at the foot of my bed looking at me like he stands at the end of my row looking at me and oh my god, what will I do if he's standing there looking at me and what if that piece of white macaroni is on his face, what if it jumped from Mother Vivian's face to his face when they kissed and what if Mother Vivian forgets to buy more vanilla wafers and there's nothing for breakfast, what if she forgets to lay out my lunch money and there's nothing to eat all day and what if Mr. W's car breaks down and he doesn't pick me up for school this morning, what if I open my door and he's still out there laying on top of Mother Vivian and she's dead and then Mr. W takes me home to live with him and I have to spend all day every day with him, even Saturday and Sunday and all summer....*
Rebecca forces her eyes open. Thank goodness Mr. W isn't standing at the foot of her bed watching her. She extends one bare leg from under the thin sheet, then the other, slowly pulls the sheet back. She hugs the long-sleeved tee shirt she wears to bed every night close in the cool morning air. It's the only thing that remains from Father Chad. At least Mother Vivian tells her Chad is her father, and he lived with them until Rebecca was in third grade. That is more than a year ago and the t-shirt is the only thing he left Rebecca to remember him by.
She can still see his face that last morning when he tip-toes into her room early before Mother Vivian awakens and starts screaming again. That's all Mother Vivian did that week, scream at Father Chad.

6

"I'm outta here, kid, I just can't take another day of this. I'm afraid I might…"

In her memory, Chad looks so sad and she wonders what he is so afraid of, but he stops then and hands her his favorite black tee shirt from the Barenaked Ladies concert where he first met Vivian, back in high school.

"Here kid, I want you to have this. Sorry it's worked out this way." He bends as if to hug her but stops and only tousles her sleep-wild hair. "Good luck, kid."

These are the last words he speaks to her. "Good luck, kid."

Rebecca pushes the memory aside, worrying again, wondering if she'd even recognize him in a crowd or would he look just like one of the faceless men who walk through Mother Vivian's bedroom door since he's gone. She wishes his smell was still in the shirt like when he'd given it to her, the sweet aroma of sweat, beer and cigarettes that she associates with him.

Vivian meets Pete Patterson at Pirate's Pub in Paisley, a hopping juke joint on the edge of the Ocala National Forest. One short stop from nowhere. After Chad leaves, Vivian longs for a man to rescue her. Rebecca prays for a fairy godmother like the one Cinderella has. It is the only way she can imagine surviving her life with Mother Vivian.

"Call me Vi, rhymes with high." Vivian walks up to the bar, smiles, pops her gum, slithers onto the empty stool next to Pete.

Pete is kind, takes Rebecca with them once on a date. Red Lobster is the best. She eats seven cheese biscuits and Mother Vivian can't stop her. "Uncle" Pete tries so hard that night Rebecca wants to imagine him as "Father" Pete.

"Close only counts in horseshoes and hand grenades." Mr. W often repeats this to his students, and Rebecca can see now how it is true.

Amado Mendez, construction supervisor of a crew of nineteen Mexican illegals, soon replaces Pete. "Roofers do a job in a day, in and out." Amado likes to smack his right fist into his left palm as he says this, an action Vivian finds irresistible. Amado's tenure is even briefer than Pete's. After that Friday night when he doesn't call, doesn't pound on her door late at night, swaggering drunk, Vivian cries for days. Not showing up for her waitress job at the Sunrise Grill for a busy Sunday breakfast rush is all it takes for the frazzled owner to fire her. Vivian drinks even more after that, sobering only to make it to the liquor store and grocery without being arrested for DUI. It is not a good summer, that first one after Father Chad leaves.

Rebecca knows other kids have mothers who give them what she learns in school is a *hearty breakfast*. "Why can't we have oatmeal for breakfast?" she asks Mother Vivian on one of their weekly grocery raids.

"Oatmeal!" Vivian snorts. "Oatmeal is for old people, Beck." Rebecca is too old to sit in the child seat of the squeaky grocery cart, but she is small for her age and no one in Sav-a-Lot pays much attention to the skinny blonde chick or her frail looking child as they bump and squeak through the store, buying one economy size box of vanilla wafers, a box of store brand tea, two bags of potato chips, fruit roll-ups for Rebecca, then head off to Walgreen's Liquor for several bottles of cheap Smirnoff vodka while it's still on sale.

The beginning days of fourth grade, Mr. Witherspoon pays special attention to Rebecca. He assigns her a seat right in front of his desk, knows her name before he knows anyone else's, smiles at her when he looks up from grading worksheets. By the end of the week, he touches her shoulder as he passes. Rebecca knows most of the kids think Mr. Witherspoon is a creep and a fat ass. News like that spreads fast in the classroom.

Friday evening when Mr. Witherspoon shows up at her door in jeans and a polo shirt, Rebecca fears she's done something so terrible it warrants a home visit. A home visit is the worst thing a teacher can do to you. None of the kids talk about it when it happens.

The touching starts right after the Christmas holiday. Mr. W travels back to family in New Jersey, and the nightly visits for cocktails and the evening meal don't resume even though school has been in session for nearly two weeks. He still picks her up each morning and drops her off in the afternoon, but he no longer comes in for cocktails.

Vivian doesn't seem to notice Mr. W's not being there. Rebecca wonders if Mother Vivian would miss *her* if one day she just didn't come home from school. Vivian takes a nightly walk around the corner to the Highway Inn Saloon, so Rebecca has every evening to watch whatever she wants on TV. Eventually she ventures around her own corner, learns to walk to the Handy Way after dark, spends the money she takes from Mother Vivian's purse and hoards in her backpack where she keeps Father Chad's shirt.

She buys macaroni and cheese packets, microwave popcorn, sometimes even a piece of fruit that Mr. Patel hangs in a wire basket by the cash register. Mr. Patel runs the store at night and he is always nice to her, learns her name, always asks how she is doing. Sometimes late at night he gives her an overripe apple or banana from the basket without making her pay.

Rebecca wonders if that's what a grandfather might do, wonders if she has a grandfather somewhere.

At first, the touching is innocent. "Hello, Rebecca, how are you this fine day?" He touches her shoulder like he does nearly every day. Familiar pats, neutral pats, until one day his hand lingers, moves up and down her back, across her shoulders. Then that afternoon in the car he places his hand on her knee, like he used to do to Mother Vivian. Not a long touch, just a fleeting pat on bare skin under her skirt, a squeeze just above her knee. She tries to make herself small and invisible against the door, like the man in the old black and white movie she watched on TV last night. The man who can only be seen when he wraps himself in clothing, like a mummy in reverse.

Rebecca's friendship with Mr. Patel develops one apple, one banana at a time. Mr. Patel is old and he doesn't really run the store like Rebecca thinks, but he works there at night for his son-in-law. Mr. Patel likes it that way because then he doesn't have to be at home with his daughter and her ambitious, demanding husband. Yes, it is much better to work the twelve-hour night shift, six to six, even though it means he is tired all the time and spends most of his non-working hours sleeping. He looks forward to Rebecca's visits, worries on the infrequent nights she doesn't come into the busy store.

Mr. Patel's daughter Supria's baby boy died from a sudden infection last year and with him her own joie de vivre. The heartbreak is more that Mr. Patel can witness and, though he longs to help her, he's learned there is nothing he can do to lessen the pain. He misses their carefree relationship. Rebecca's appearance late at night in the convenience store warms his aching heart. Rebecca gradually loses the grayness she had when she first walked into the Handy Way. Her friendship with Mr. Patel blossoms.

Mexicans and local boys use the dark side of the parking lot to deal drugs. She hears the kids who hang outside the store say, "Old Mr. Patel's half blind, he don't see what goes on out here." In the shadows, money passes hand to hand, packages slip unnoticed from pocket to pocket. Rebecca gives the boys a wide berth, walks eyes forward "with a purpose" as she has seen on a late night informercial selling personal protection pepper spray canisters. *Always walk with a purpose and the attacker will not choose you.* Going to visit Mr. Patel has become her purpose.

Mother Vivian is rarely sober now. Rebecca wonders if Mother Vivian makes late night trips to meet the boys outside the store, but she hopes to never see her there. Vivian sleeps all day while Rebecca is at school, no longer wakes even to prepare the morning pearl tea and vanilla wafer that has been her one concession to motherhood. Rebecca finds she can bring home an apple from Mr. Patel, prepare a bowl of microwave oatmeal, also from Mr. Patel, add a small carton of orange juice, and she has a *hearty breakfast*, one like she's learned about in school.

Mr. Patel stops charging for her purchases. He begins saving things back for her. An unblemished banana, the latest box of chocolate donuts from the Entenmann's delivery which they share at night along with a carton of chocolate milk before Rebecca returns home.

Even though he would like to, Mr. Patel can't leave the Handy Way unattended to walk her home. "I'm sorry, Rebecca, but Krishna only knows what those hoodlums will do if they see I am not standing here." He makes sure she leaves each night before ten. For

Valentine's day he gives her a pre-paid cell phone with instructions to tell no one, especially Mother Vivian. "You will be calling me once you're safely locking your door." They use a secret code, letting it ring once, then hanging up. "This way we will not be spending any money." He smiles and tousles her hair.

One windy March afternoon, Mr. Patel wakes early and walks to the nearby elementary school Rebecca attends. He has the intention of escorting her home. Mr. Patel has not officially met Mr. W who is still doggedly driving Rebecca to and from school.

Rebecca is alone in the classroom, the rest of the class dismissed an hour ago. Another fifteen minutes before Mr. W can leave and Rebecca will be free from his creepy looks and his sweaty touches.

When Rebecca tells him she wants to walk to school, she no longer wants him to pick her up in the morning, Mr. W shakes his head and stares at his feet. "It's the least I can do for you, Rebecca, it's my Christian duty, what with your mother being what she's become." He clicks his tongue the way he does when someone in class irritates him. "The Good Lord wouldn't take kindly to me letting you walk out there by yourself. Why, what if…." Mr. W looks her up and down. She forces her hands to remain at her sides, unclenched and not pulling on the hem of her short pink skirt. "No way, young lady, no way will I abandon you to the wolves out there who would just love to eat you up." His fat hand pushes back a lock of his stringy black hair. "The Good Lord's told me to do this, and that's what I'm gonna do. Now go back to your seat and do your homework."

That first afternoon when Rebecca spots Mr. Patel, it is too late to go to him. He looks so lonely, standing outside the entrance, all the yellow busses loaded and gone, only the teachers' cars in the parking lot. Rebecca doesn't see Mr. Patel until Mr. W opens the passenger car door of his dirty white Ford Taurus, and she looks one last time toward the entrance of the building. Mr. Patel has been watching her, he lifts one arm and waves. She feels Mr. W's knuckles on her shoulder guiding her into the car and does not wave back.

She can hardly wait for Mother Vivian to go out that night. She runs into the store breathless and doesn't wait for him to finish with a customer buying lottery tickets. "Was that you?"

Mr. Patel nods for her to mind her manners, wait her turn. Rebecca is learning a lot from Mr. Patel, patience is one of those things.

"Who is that man whose car you were entering?" he asks once the customer has pocketed the wad of paper tickets.

"Mr. Witherspoon. He's my teacher. He gives me a ride to school and home again. He used to date Mother Vivian, but not anymore."

Mr. Patel frowns. He recognizes the hefty man from his nightly visits to the store, long before Rebecca walks over from the apartment. He comes in, buys Little Debbie's, Twinkies, Cheetos, that kind of thing, and beer, always lots of beer, at least a twelve pack each night. Mr. Patel's head hurts from wondering how such a man can be a teacher, an elementary teacher of young students.

"Well, I don't want you riding again with him. I'm walking you to school tomorrow and I'll be there walking you home." Rebecca accepts the apple he hands her, along with a new box of microwave oatmeal. The bell tied to the door rings and Mr. Patel steps back behind the counter. "Now go along home, young lady. It's Friday night and this is no place for you." He shooes her toward the door. "Don't forget calling me when you get home." Already he is searching the rack for cigarettes and handing the customer some change.

Seconds before the bell rings Monday morning, Rebecca slips into her seat. Mr. W glares at her. Rebecca manages to be first at the door for lunch, finds a seat behind a column in the back of the cafeteria, hopes Mr. W won't spot her sitting alone. When the last afternoon bell rings, she is first out the door.

It is Wednesday before Mr. W calls her name and tells her to remain after class. "Where have you been, Rebecca? The Lord's not happy about me not giving you a ride to and from school."

Rebecca stands before his desk, keeps her eyes on her dirty pink flip-flops. "I don't want a ride to school anymore, Mr. Witherspoon."

"Now Rebecca, I told you the Lord spoke to me. He wants me to protect you from that riff-raff out there. The Lord expects you to ride to school with me, or he's not gonna be happy with you, and you don't want the Lord being unhappy with you, now do you?" He moves to stand behind her, places his beefy hands on her thin shoulders, massages her back with his fingers. Rebecca flinches when he starts making the noise she remembers from those times on the couch with Mother Vivian, a sort of low animal sound, somewhere between a growl and a moan.

"No!" Rebecca wrenches from his grasp, lurches toward the classroom door, runs down the stairs toward the outside and freedom. The heavy steel door slams.

Rebecca stops running when she reaches Mr. Patel waiting next to the battered hibiscus. An earlier conversation echoes in her head. "Always in such a hurry, you are, young lady. In my day, we weren't hurrying so, and young ladies were never hurrying."

Mr. Patel's face wrinkles in a smile and he bends to remove her backpack. "How was your day, young lady?" Rebecca doesn't turn to look up at the second story window to see if Mr. W is standing there watching; she can feel his eyes against her back. In a sudden move, Rebecca grabs Mr. Patel's sleeve and pulls him forward. "You're the best part of my day, Mr. Patel. Absolutely the best part."

For the rest of that week, Mr. Witherspoon ignores Rebecca entirely, but with each passing day her sense of unease increases. When he commands her to remain after class Friday afternoon, her stomach flops with anxiety. The years of living with Mother Vivian keep it from showing on her face.

She watches Mr. Witherspoon waddle to the classroom door and turn the lock. Sweat breaks out on her upper lip and the hours she spends sharpening his pencils and cleaning his whiteboard come back in a rush. She bites her lip as he walks across the room, stands behind her. She tenses as he places his beefy hands on her shoulders, feels a tear form as those hands move up and down across her back, down her buttocks, under her skirt to touch her in that place where the policewoman who spoke to the all-girls life skills class said no adult should ever touch her.

Suddenly Rebecca feels Mr. Patel standing behind her, strong and sure. She remembers the face of the uniformed policewoman, remembers the woman's sharp blue eyes drilling into her very soul, teaching her about safety and self-esteem. She remembers Cinderella's fairy godmother and the magic pumpkin that carries Cinderella to the ball where she meets Prince Charming.

Rebecca takes a deep breath, exhales, pulls away from Mr. W, stands and draws herself to her full height. She smoothes the back of her skirt down, turns to face him. He is the color of a mottled plum, plump and unhealthy, his eyes squinty and pig-like in his fat round face. His chin drops to his chest and he refuses to meet her gaze.

"You're a teacher, Mr. Witherspoon, and you're behaving like a bad man. You were a bad man with Mother Vivian and then you left her. You didn't even give her that Christmas present you promised. Teachers are supposed to help their students. They're not supposed to touch them where you touched me. They're not supposed to yell at us. They're not supposed to...." she falters, searching for just the right word.

Mr. Patel's voice sounds in her mind. A clear memory of him talking about Mr. Witherspoon surfaces. "A teacher is a person having a lot of duty." Mr. Patel was unusually serious that night. "A teacher is someone you are looking up to, someone you are admiring at all times. A teacher is someone who is caring for you, even sometimes when you are not caring for yourself. Being a teacher is one of the most important jobs we have today."

"You're a fake!" Words burst from Rebecca like water bursting from a balloon dropped onto a cement sidewalk from a second story window. She leans forward, surprised to see a tear trailing down his spongy purple cheek. "You are not a nice person, Mr. Witherspoon," she draws out his name so it sounds like a snake hissing, unseen, in the weeds behind the Handy Way. "You are not a nice person and you will never touch me again, do you hear me?" She waits for Mr. Witherspoon to look at her, to nod his head in agreement, to make some sign he's understood.

His faded yellow shirt is spotted with sauce stains from the spaghetti in today's school lunch. A tear drops into a dark red blotch. She stares at the cartoon faces of smiling children that cover his wrinkled tie.

"If you ever touch me again, put one finger on me, I'll tell everyone who will listen. Do you hear me?"

Mr. Witherspoon seems to fold in on himself, a bowl of blubbering fat—nameless, faceless, hopeless. He walks to his desk, sits heavily in the swivel chair, turns to face the whiteboard. "You're dismissed, Rebecca. Dismissed." Sobbing now, he cannot continue. The sound is even worse than the primitive growl he made when he touched her.

Rebecca lets the wooden classroom door close and walks down the stairs to where Mr. Patel waits faithfully by the shabby hibiscus.

His smile thaws her soul, her heart regains its rhythm. She knows what happened today, and she knows Mr. Patel is her friend and he is waiting for her just as he had been yesterday and he would be tomorrow.

"How was your day, young lady?"

"It was a good day, Mr. Patel. It was a very good day and this is my favorite part of every day, when you're waiting here to walk me home."

For the first time, after he removes her backpack and slings it over his narrow shoulders, Rebecca takes his hand. He smiles down at her, paces his steps to her smaller ones. "And tell me, young lady, what were you learning in school today?"

THE SKULL

Smooth, polished skull.
Good teeth. Can't have been too old.
Jaw hanging open.
Did he die screaming?

Vertebrae attached to the neck,
held in place by a plastic rod,
nearly invisible.
Same pearly white as the skull.

Funny to look at it this way.
No sign of what kind of car he drove,
how much money he made.
Was he happy?

Look again at that open jaw.
Maybe not happy on this day.
Was he black, white, red, brown, yellow?
After it's all over, does it matter?

What remains from a life?
More than the frame that supported it,
More than the few cents worth of minerals
that composed it.

Turn it over.
Look inside.
Wonder what was in that cranial cavity,
now void of all but space.

Then see something.
A black speck just under the cheekbone.
Tiny, but something.

Pull the old metal encased magnifying glass
from the creaky desk.

Hold it close.
Squint.
Really tiny.

Then I see it.

Made in China.

A SATISFIED MAN

There were only two things in his life Marion Pryor had to do better. He had to make more paintings and then he had to sell them. Fast. All of them, as many as he could paint. That was the only way he could see to keep Laverne off his back.

Last Saturday not one of his paintings sold. He waited all day, under his umbrella, eating boiled peanuts he'd brought from home. Waited. Not one car stopped. He was scared to face Laverne that night and was too ashamed to even stop by Curley's house and tell him about the day.

This morning before he left, Laverne had shot him one of those looks. One of those looks that said, 'Now don't be coming back here empty-handed tonight like you done last week.' It was a look he hated.

He'd pondered on the boiled peanuts. This Friday night he packed wood for the fire, cook stand and kettle, and ten pounds of green peanuts.

He would not come home empty-handed again. He had no choice. Laverne had given him *that look* and *that* was *that*. Peanuts, paintings, he'd sell *something* to bring in some money.

21

On Sunday, Marion knew if he didn't have a crisp ten dollar bill to lay in Brother Johnson's collection plate, he'd never hear the end of Laverne's carping. And Sunday, well Sunday was another bone of contention between him and Laverne. "It's jest a day wasted, darlin', when I could be sitting out there selling my paintings."

"You know what Brother Johnson says, 'bout working on Sunday. The good Lord didn't do it, and you don't need to be doing it neither." The subject was closed, at least in Laverne's mind.

Marion headed out at first light. He'd filled the back seat with seven large, brightly colored Florida landscape paintings. He found a good spot along the highway not too far out of town, had a little shade where he could cook his boiled peanuts, display his paintings, and maybe even read a chapter or two in the Bible that Laverne insisted he carry with him. At least it didn't look like rain.

Painting was just another way to support his family and he loved it, the painting, the selling, the coming and goings of it all. Just as he loved Laverne's faith in the Lord. On Sunday mornings, Marion felt good inside when he was able to drop a hard-earned ten dollar bill in Brother Johnson's collection plate. When he painted, the feeling guided his hands. Beauty and grace and brilliant color in everything, it all poured out.

Peanuts smelling good, day warm but not yet hot, the first truck pulled in mid-morning. Marion got a good feeling inside as he watched an old man—farmer's straw hat, bib overalls—carefully shut the truck door and stand looking at the paintings. "Mighty colorful," he nodded toward Marion.

"Yessir," Marion answered. "Just like some of those sunsets the good Lord sends us."

The old farmer looked over to the simmering kettle of peanuts.

Marion nodded toward the peanuts, never raising his eyes. "Fresh from Georgia from my cousin's farm."

"Georgia." The farmer hadn't moved, just stooped closer to the painting—a flock of white ibis flying into a bright orange sunset. Palm trees.

"Yessir. Care to try some?" Marion dipped a small tin cup into the peanuts, handed it across.

The old man shuffled and gazed at the paintings, letting the peanuts cool in the cup. "How much?"

"The peanut's, fifty cents, the painting's twenty-five dollars."

The old man continued to stare at the birds flying into the orange and purple sunset. "Seen one like that the night my wife's pa died. Twenty years ago. Ain't never forgot it, neither." He turned back to Marion. "Take a double bag o' them goobers, young man."

Marion carefully filled the brown paper bags with steaming peanuts. "One dollar, sir." He handed over the peanuts, accepted the crumpled bill, nodded, kept his smile to himself.

First sale of the day and still well before noon.

By one that afternoon Marion had counted fifty-seven cars driven by; nine had stopped, all for peanuts. Marion had counted twenty-three Chevys, two Studebakers ten Buicks, two Cadillacs and twenty Fords. Thirty pickups, twenty-five sedans, and two woody station wagons.

Counting was something Marion did to keep his mind from going bad on him. He counted everything. Cars along the road, the number of bright yellow dresses in church, hats with feathered plumes, how many crackers his son Willy liked to eat in a bowl of steaming chili, how many brush strokes it took to paint a Poinciana tree.

He'd never told Laverne about the counting. She'd enlighten him by saying he ought to be reciting some verse from the Bible. And he'd tried that, mostly when

23

they were first married and he tried hard to please her. He wasn't good at remembering Bible verses, but he was good at numbers, good at counting, and it kept his mind settled. So he counted.

Fifty-eight. Fifty-nine. Number sixty stopped, a station wagon driven by a bedraggled woman and a load of kids. She bought two bags of peanuts and yelled, "You youngins' share or I'll smack you till your butt burns worsn'a red hot chili pepper." She left a cloud of dust when she pulled back out onto the hard road.

By mid-afternoon, fourteen more cars and seventeen trucks had passed. Three of the cars and nine of the trucks had stopped for boiled peanuts. Only the dregs remained.

Marion was grateful for that.

Then that same truck driven by the farmer who'd stopped earlier in the day pulled over. The old farmer sat behind the wheel without moving for so long that Marion started to wonder.

Finally the rusted truck door creaked and Marion watched the man's shadow on the ground as he used the door for support to slowly climb down. Marion kept his eyes down. He was used to that and was keen at observing small details in others. He knew when they wanted to buy something. He listened, he watched. When the time was right, he played his highest card. Ninety-nine times out of a hundred, it worked like a charm.

The old man stopped in front of the painting he'd admired earlier. Marion stared at the ground, waited for him to make the first move. Eventually the old man turned his head toward Marion, said "Them were some good boiled peanuts."

Marion raised his eyes half-way. "Thank you, sir. Glad you enjoyed 'em."

Another lengthy silence passed.

"I been thinking about this painting all day. My wife's father dying and all. The sunset that night. I've never been able to get that picture outta my head, you know, and now here it is." His straw hat tipped toward the painting. "I done thought about this all afternoon, till finally I hears this voice in my head saying, 'Marion, if you don't buy this painting for your good wife, Lucille, you 're just a damn fool.' So I stopped."

Now Marion looked him straight in the eye and said, "Marion, sir? Your name is Marion?"

The farmer nodded, never moved his eyes from the painting.

"Well, that's my name too, sir. Marion Pryor and I certainly would love for you to buy that painting." He moved one step closer.

Finally the old man looked him in the face. "My Lucille will love this. She's been ailing lately. Maybe this will bring her some sunshine." Without even haggling, he handed Marion twenty-five dollars. "Keep on painting, Marion Pryor. These are just swell."

Just after the o'dark-thirty, Marion pulled down the sandy lane leading to his cabin nestled between two orange groves. He had fifty dollars in his pocket. Ten dollars for Brother Johnson, enough to keep Laverne happy for another week, food for the kids, money for more paint and Upson board.

Marion Pryor was a satisfied man.

C – –

It was summer 1967.
The corn was tall
and I was still green.
It was an elective,

a summer course to fill a void.
It was the right time of day
so I chose Home Economics 231,
Marriage and Family.

Ward and June had not been my parents,
and I was the wrong gender to be Beaver.
Maybe this would create a new picture.
It was a term paper, any topic you chose

in a class extolling the virtues of a traditional marriage
and a traditional family in a traditional world.
There were nightly images of body bags,
images of Berkeley and the Beatles,

images of screaming and tear gas.
I had no words for the madness,
the fear, the denial, the unexpressed grief.
Betty Freidan changed my life with

The Feminine Mystique, proof that
women had been sold a bill of goods.

I knew, I'd seen it first-hand.
I'd known duty and obligation and little thanks.
I'd worked wanting praise and received only criticism.
I'd had enough of duty.
I needed to fly.
There were roles, constrictions, rules keeping me there.

I found support for change in my yearning for freedom
and I read and I wrote and went to class at 11.
I felt better for that.
Eventually the paper returned

as pure and white as the day I'd turned it in.
Only one mark,
in red–small, small print, bottom right.
C minus minus.

I can still feel the anger surge.

HOMELAND SECURITY

Damn. Principal Brown would call a faculty meeting this afternoon. I need to leave early again today to take my ninety-two-year old mother back to the Government ID office. We'd been there yesterday to renew her photo ID. That's what you have when you're too old to drive but still need to prove you're a card-carrying American citizen.

Mom and I made it to the office yesterday just after four. Should have been plenty of time for her to be photographed, pay the thirty-five dollars for the new ID, and we're on our way.

"No ma'am." from the twenty-something blond behind the counter. "The Office of Homeland Security now requires that anyone whose ID has expired or who doesn't have a current driver's license, provide their current tax bill, a stamped birth certificate, and their last three month's utility bills. You must provide the originals."

"My mom has lived in this county every one of her ninety-two years. She probably went to school with your great-grandfather."

"No ma'am," the blue eyes were sweetly innocent. "My great-grandfather lived in Minnesota all his life."

"Yeah, but can you document that," I muttered.

"Ma'am?" Miss twnety-something had that look on her face, the one I've seen so often since Dad's death.

"Never mind." My ninety-two year-old mom looks nothing like a bearded Arab terrorist, but reality and common sense have lost a lot of ground to Homeland Security.

I pull out my cell phone, call Mom, tell her we'll have to make the trip to get her ID renewed tomorrow. Emergency Faculty Meeting this afternoon.

"Yes, dear, I understand. I'll just take off these good clothes and hang them up for tomorrow. I've got lots of room in my closet since you were over last week and threw out all your Dad's stuff."

"Mom...." I stop myself just in time. "Sorry Mom, got to go. Love you."

CNN blares in the hallway as I walk down to Room 114. A young Hispanic reporter interviewing a distant family member of the young Wisconsin high school student who killed his school principal, injured thirty-five classmates. The study hall was cordoned off with yellow crime scene tape. Kid came to school carrying an old AK 47 assault rifle, belonged to his dad. I ignore the noise and continue my mental grocery list. Chad is bringing a friend home for dinner and I hadn't done the shopping yesterday. Another Homeland Security casualty.

The room buzzes with the usual end of the day chit chat. Who'd been caught smoking pot in the third floor girl's bathroom, who wasn't eligible to play in tomorrow night's football game—too many absences. Turn your money in for the lottery pool, cause Nancy in the front office says she's not floating any more loans, and she means it this time.

Mr. Brown clears his throat. "I've been on the phone with Superintendent Cowlin off and on all afternoon, and I just want to give you a heads up on what's coming down the pike." Several people groan, the room quiets.

"The Office of Homeland Security has recommended to the President that in order to keep our schools safe, beginning next school year all administrators, teachers, and school staff are to report for duty armed."

Gasps, hoots, a few curse words. I feel the Homeland Security boulder drop into my gut, my eyes burn. Blinking back tears, I try to breathe. All around me people are talking, but all I hear is "Pot roast or pork chops, pot roast or pork chops, pot roast or pork chops."

Mr. Brown clears his throat, waits for silence. "I have a prepared statement from HomeLand Security that I am to read to you.

"To make our schools safe for our students to learn, all options should be on the table. Israel and Thailand have well-trained teachers carrying weapons and keeping their children safe from harm. It can work just as well here in the United States.

"Beginning in January, each administrator, teacher, and staff member of every school district, will be assigned to a firearms safety class. Initially only sixty hours of training will be required. The purchase of appropriate firearms will be authorized for payroll deduction."

Loud buzzing, like mad hornets, dims the pot roast or pork chop refrain in my head.

"Each school board will designate appropriate training sites and appropriate vendors for the purchase of required firearms. In addition to the required firearm training, all school personnel will wear designated uniforms and other appropriate gear. Each administrator and teacher will be issued an Internet ready Personal Digital Assistant to provide instant access to Homeland Security for emergency situations. PDAs will be provided free of charge and training programs will be offered at reduced rates.

"Additional information will be provided through the Office of Homeland Security to each school district in the United States within the next month."

I look down at my notepad, notice wet spots, dab my face with a tissue, hope no one is looking at me. Several male coaches are laughing and slapping one another on the back. "Yeah, we can have some fun now."

Pot roast or pork chops, pot roast or pork chops. I tear off a dry portion of my notepad, write pork chops, stuff the paper in my pocket, look at my watch.

Ten more minutes, he can only keep us ten more minutes. I'll make it to Publix before the rush.

CRACKER JACKS

Any more, I don't buy Cracker Jacks.
The last box was stale.

Jacks clinging together for safety,
sticking to the sides of the box.
Eight tasteless, limp peanuts
nestling at the bottom.

The prize? A tear apart paper puzzle.
The Quaker, Susan B. Anthony.
The woman who devoted her life to promoting
women's suffrage, but didn't live to see it.

Her voice reaches me through this
cellophane world of murder and mayhem.
Sirens and orange road construction barrels
mark my boundaries.

I wish, as she must have, for peace, equality among
humanity.
I wait, as she must have, for these things to
manifest in our world.

I vote, but
I no longer buy Cracker Jacks.
You see, there's too much history in there
and I am not prepared.

SAFE HAVEN

It all started with the History channel, damn them. Program after program on the coming Apocalypse. The Apocalypse according to the Bible, the Apocalypse according to Nostradamus, the Mayans, the Hindus, the Hopi. The Apocalypse and the End of the World.

My husband Hank was glued to the damn History channel for hours on end, neglecting the dog, neglecting the trash, the yard, absorbed by the coming End of the World. He filled the house with books from the library, read all of Nostradamus, at least three different translations, studied the tomes of Isaac Newton, read *The Egyptian Book of the Dead*, *The Tibetan Book of the Dead*. Books were everywhere and all he could think about was the End Times. What the hell did the Egyptians and the Tibetans know about 2012 anyway? Those books were written centuries ago, before computers, before the Internet. They didn't even have electricity, for heaven's sake. How could they possibly know what would happen on December 21, 2012?

After several months of this, Hank decided to build our Safe Haven. Said a bomb shelter like his dad built back in the 50s, was passé. The Russians had fallen from power and it was unlikely the Pakistanis could ever accumulate enough plutonium to make a nuclear bomb, and even if they did, it was doubtful any of those Chinese missiles were accurate enough to hit the broad side of a barn, much less the United Damned States of America.

Hank started making his plans. He'd excavate under the garage and build our Safe Haven, somewhere we could survive the coming disaster so accurately predicated by the ancient and dead sages of the world. He found some old drafting tools at a yard sale, bought the drafting table that went with it, and started planning. A week later he unrolled the vellum sheets and covered the dining room table.

"This is it, honey, this is what's going to save us." I nodded mutely and went to the kitchen to make another pot of coffee. Along with the end of the world obsession came his obsession for coffee. Morning, noon, and night, coffee, coffee, and more coffee. He stopped eating meat, ate only brown rice and vegetables. "It's important to give your body time to adjust to the coming changes. There won't be any animals left after the Apocalypse, so you might as well get used to it now." Bags of brown rice started stacking up against the back garage wall. Fifty pounds bags, floor to ceiling. "At least we won't starve to death," he smiled as he carried in another fifty-pound bag. "May not be gourmet, but we'll be fed."

The excavation went on all summer, wheelbarrow after wheelbarrow of dirt filling the back yard. By July, we were surrounded by a mountainous berm, and I could no longer see the neighbors' house. It was about this same time that H1N1 was in the headlines, blaring from CNN morning, noon and night. "It's nature's way," he'd shake his head. "Nature's way of getting rid of the weak, the unfit, the god-damned minorities that are the ruination of our society." Hank had all the answers.

One morning he came back from his shopping run with several bags of protective white masks. "I want you to start wearing one of these every time you leave the house," he announced. I looked at him, removed one of the paper masks from its plastic bag, took off my glasses and placed it on my face.

"I can't breathe." I tried adjusting my glasses so I could see. I ripped the mask off and placed it back in the bag, went to the kitchen, made another pot of coffee. The bags continued to pile up on the shelf next to the brown rice.

"I couldn't live if something happened to you, honey. I want you to wear one of these if you leave the property."

"If I leave the property?" I didn't like the sound of that one bit. Already I could no longer see the neighbors, he'd had the land line taken out, disconnected the service on my cell phone. "We need to cut back, honey, more important things to spend our money on."

A few days later he sold my car. "I can't bear the thought of losing you. What if some damned drunken Puerto Rican kills you out on 441? I can't bear it."

The next thing I knew, he'd cancelled my Gold's Gym membership. I went in on Tuesday morning as usual, and my card wouldn't scan. "Sorry," Sherri behind the counter said. "Your husband called yesterday and cancelled your membership." Same thing with my yoga class. I arrived Thursday morning to be told by Yogini Kataya that Hank had stopped by yesterday and cancelled my membership. "He said you were going out of town," she frowned as she said this, "going to care for a sick relative up north somewhere."

The tears didn't start until I was in the parking lot back in Hank's Honda. Damn him, he'd already cancelled our Internet, the phones, and the newspaper. I was becoming more and more isolated and I didn't know what to do.

I made a pot of coffee, walked down the wooden steps to the Safe Haven carrying a cup. My hands were shaking so that only about half remained by the time I was standing on the packed earthen floor. I blinked in the fluorescent glare of the bulbs strung across the ceiling. "Color-balanced," he announced. "We won't be seeing the sun for a few years, so it's important that your body absorb a balanced light spectrum while we wait." He looked up from his drilling and smiled. "I brought your yoga mat down for you, dear."

I set the coffee on the bench next to him and walked back upstairs.

He picked up the mail from the mailbox each day. I never received any. By September I stopped leaving the house entirely. Once my friend Cara pulled in the drive, but Hank was out the door, and she was pulling away before I could even put on my clothes. I'd taken to spending more and more time in bed, staring up at the ceiling. At first Hank would bring me copies of the *Egyptian* and *Tibetan Books of the Dead*, but when I didn't read them, he carried the tomes back down to the Safe Haven. I rarely left the bedroom, stopped taking showers, almost never combed my hair.

One morning when he brought my steaming cup of black coffee, he sat down on the bed next to me. "I'm doing this for you, honey. I couldn't bear it if anything happened to you. I'm doing all this for you." He reached over and touched my face, folded a piece of stringy hair behind my ear. I rolled over, pulled the blanket over my head, and sobbed. My teeth clenched when he patted my trembling shoulder. "You'll see, honey, I'm doing this all for you."

I didn't leave the bedroom for a month.

By now I was eating nothing except brown rice and drinking only black coffee. I slept fitfully, when I slept at all. I saw Hank only when he brought me food. I never left the bedroom and he'd moved into the Safe Haven. "I want to make sure everything is snug and warm, dear. I don't want you to be uncomfortable. After all we'll be in there for a long, long time."

I have no idea how much time passed, but one day I came to some awareness that I was in the shower and Hank was standing beside me. I struggled to stand on my own. I felt weak and unsteady. "This is the big day, dear." Hank poured shampoo into my hair and began massaging my scalp. "The Safe Haven is finished and I want to show it to you."

Mutely I let him shower me, dress me in a now oversized pair of sweatpants and an old tee shirt. I'd lost so much weight, the clothes hung from my emaciated frame. He helped me down the dark stairs, sat me carefully on a wooden stool at the bottom. When the color-balanced lights flashed on, I was blinded. "Taa–dah!" His voice boomed in my ear. "It's ready! What do you think?"

I managed to nod in his direction before I wobbled to my feet and step-by-single-step climbed back up the stairs, shuffled down the hall to my bedroom. I couldn't think. I'd stopped thinking weeks ago, I had no idea what month it was.

One day I awoke in a strange bed and Hank was lying beside me. I could see nothing, only hear his rhythmic breathing. When he felt me stir, he announced, "It's time dear, we're here." I turned my head to the wall and wished I were dead. Maybe I was dead. For a brief second I regretted not reading one of those damned Books of the Dead he'd given me. Maybe I'd have a clue what was happening. I tried not to move, not to even breathe.

ONE YEAR LATER

Hank breezed into Froggers with a thin blond on his arm, a thin blond thirty years younger and light-years dimmer in intellect. The waitress led them to a corner table, soon delivered draft beer and loaded potato skins. "Tell me about your meeting with the wedding planner," he smiled into her carefully made-up face.

"It was soooo cool," Vanessa reached for his hands. "I wish you'd gone with me."

"No honey," Hank replied, "you know I had to meet with that sales rep. The store is set to open next week."

"Why can't you wait 'till after the wedding to open the store?" Vanessa was appealing when she pouted, it was all he could do to resist.

"Now, honey, you know it's important to get the store open. So many people want the new line of organic food. All that hype about genetic engineeriing has scared the bejesus out of folks. I've got to keep the customers' needs first." Hank sipped a beer and popped a potato skin in his mouth. "And you know, it was Cindy's dream to open this store, it was the last thing she said to me before she died. 'Hank, you've got to open that store. People need to eat, and they need to eat well.'"

Vanessa tried to look sympathetic. She'd heard all about the well-meaning Cindy, her interest in organic foods, how once she was diagnosed with cancer, she'd made Hank promise to open a store, that he wouldn't let this terrible thing happen to another woman. And of course, Hank made that promise "If it's the last thing I do, dear. If it's the last thing I do."

Vanessa knew when to keep her mouth shut, she'd learned that from Milo, the guy she'd dated before Hank came along. She still had a ridge of scar tissue along the inside of her lower lip from the time Milo'd busted her for arguing with him. That's how she knew Hank was the one. He'd come into her salon to be styled. "My wife's funeral is tomorrow. Want to look my best." His smile was so sincere her heart melted right that instant. She'd rarely looked at another man since.

"It's what Cindy would have wanted, dear," he told her as he held out the small diamond ring, looking up at her from bended knees, the girls in the salon gaping at the scene. "Cindy made me promise right before she died. 'Now Hank,' she'd said, 'I don't want you to grieve, I want to you move on with your life. Find a nice young woman and marry. Maybe she'll have a couple of kids, you can raise that family you always said you wanted.'" Vanessa was so taken with Hank that she didn't see the rolling eyes of her co-workers, refused to hear their attempts to talk her out of marrying Hank. "He's thirty years older, Vanessa. What are you thinking?" "Didn't his wife just die? Her body's not even cold yet. Can't you give it some time?"

Hank cinched the deal when he took Vanessa down to the Safe Haven. "This is where she died," he whispered. "Right in this bed, right where you are now." His tears fell against the bare skin of her shoulder. He didn't make love to her like a younger man would have, didn't push her to do things she really didn't want to do, just held her, tears dropping onto her bare shoulder. She'd held him until he'd fallen asleep that night. She'd made up her mind that this was the man she'd waited for, the man who was going to make her happy.

The wedding went as planned, small, yes, but perfect. Vanessa was stunning in her white dress, tanned and fit. Hank looked handsome in his tux and only a couple of the out-of-town guests had mistaken him for her father. The honeymoon was postponed due to the store opening the next day. Hank promised to make it up to her. "Cindy always wanted me to take her to Mexico City, dear. That's where I want to take you. Our honeymoon, the beginning of our married life."

It won't be a beginning, will it, Vanessa thought, since we'll have been married for several months, but she didn't want to argue. Hank, after all, had given her everything she wanted in the wedding. The honeymoon could wait.

"Here, I want you to read this, and I've recorded a number of programs from the History Channel that I think you'll enjoy."

Vanessa looked at the book, *Nostradamus Decoded*, a thick dark volume. She wasn't much of a reader, but she carefully placed the book on the table next to her side of the bed. The History Channel, though, now that was something else. She'd hated history in high school and thought the History Channel was only for geeks. Still, she wanted to make Hank happy, so she nodded and paid attention when he showed her where the large stack of recorded dvds were stored, next to the flat screen tv.

When Hank sat next to her on the sofa that night, instructed her on which dvd to begin watching, she'd been compliant. "Here's where I want you to start, dear. The one labeled *Apocalypse 2012*. That one was Cindy's favorite."

DREAD

I watch them drag old Mrs. Anthony to the street.

Will they come for me next?

Only two of them—old men this time.
Do they send old ones for the other old ones?

Mrs. Anthony doesn't go quietly. She screeches,
scrapes, scratches, and struggles every step to the
waiting Suburban, windows black and barred.

How many remain?

I am the only young one still on my block.

How many others can there be?

It's the voting. I regret the day Mrs. Anthony took me
to register.

I'll be next. I know I will.

SATAN'S OWN CANCER

"I see ya, Miss Bible Toter. Don't be comin' here thinkin' you can be savin' me for Jesus." LeRoy spit, barely missed one of Miss Etta's tan leather lace-ups as she stood next to him on the splintered asphalt parking lot.

A tiny baby squirmed in his arms. Two young boys, eyes big and round, hung onto each baggy pant leg. Both stared open-mouthed at the large older woman their father was yelling at. Shattered glass sparkled in the sunshine, shards spattering the battered asphalt parking lot next to the abandoned liquor store.

"The hell you doin' in the 'hood? You thinking that silly Bible is gonna save you from some nutcase?" LeRoy spit again. "You outa you friggin' mind."

Miss Etta stepped through broken glass outside the crumbling concrete block building. "Where yo baby mama?"

"None of you god-damn bidness, woman. Get on away from me." LeRoy yanked the four-year old twins, Jerome and Jirard, behind him.

"They wouldn't be those corner ladies, would they?" Etta looked deep in each young boy's face, studied them hard. "Those wimmens out there solicitin', is they?"

"How you think I feed these chilrens and they mommas? I can't get no work, not with the white man's mark on me. You see these three teardrop on my face? You surely knows what they means. Three friggin' times, the Man busted me. For what? For trying to feed these chilrens? They mamas? And for what? Nothin', that's what. For being a nigger in the wrong place. Sum bitch, woman. The hell you thinkin', walking 'round here."

Miss Etta pulled her red shawl tighter around her broad shoulders. "My son be gone now, gone to Jesus." She waved a piece of orange paper like a flag. "I want to give you this, from the Believers Faith Fellowship."

LeRoy frowned, spit again. "Get that 'way from me, woman. I ain't tellin' yo again."

Miss Etta moved in closer. "You know yo' mama brung you to the Believers Faith Fellowship when you was a boy. Brung all you youngins, she did." The orange paper shook harder. "Yo mama and I was girls together. Like sisters, we was." She moved in still closer, looking up into his hardened face. "She'd be ashamed, she would, seeing you here, pimpin' yo baby mamas to feed her grans."

Just then, Takeshya, the twin's mama, sashayed up. "Why, Miss Etta! Look at you! I ain't seen you in years! Don't you look fine!"

Miss Etta smiled broadly. "Why, Takeshya. Lordy, girl. Don't *you* look fine."

The women hugged.

"Get on outta here, 'Keysha. You ain't done for today, not a bit." LeRoy handed Jerome the baby, pushed all three boys up under the barred window.

"Don't move from here, Jerome. Not a step, hear me?"

Jerome bounced the baby in his arms and smiled shyly when Miss Etta tucked an orange paper in his hand. "Keep that, son. Give it to yo' mama when she come home tonight."

"He ain't yo' son. Don't be giving him ideas that things is gonna change." LeRoy's anger was on fire, sparking. "Things ain't never gonna change, and it's just wrong to let 'em think they will."

LeRoy dwarfed Miss Etta, but she didn't back up even when he sprayed her face with spittle. She ran her fingers along the three tattooed teardrops. "I loved yo mama, LeRoy. And she loved you. It weren't her fault that God took her when he did, right when you needed her most. It were the Cancer, LeRoy. It weren't God. It weren't that she wanted to leave you and yo sisters neither. It were Satan's own Cancer."

LeRoy used his fist to rub a piece of dust from his eye. "Get on outta here. Jesus don't want nothin' to do with me. Never did."

"That's not true, son. Jesus loves you, he loves yo' chilrens and he loves they mamas. We havin' a fried chicken dinner Wednesday night at Believers Faith. It'd do them boys good to eat some home cookin'."

Miss Etta smiled at Takeysha. "Honey, take this and bring them boys for some supper on Wednesday. You'll be welcome there."

Takeysha tucked the paper in her bag, gave Miss Etta a quick kiss on the cheek, and trotted back to her spot on the corner. "See ya Sunday, Miss Etta." She glanced over at LeRoy and started walking back and forth, swinging her long legs and sashaying her hips just like he'd taught her.

Sunday was still a long ways off.

TROUBLE

Trouble arrives unannounced,
unwanted, uninvited,
crawling through the cracked
weather stripping at the back door.

Outside the kitchen window,
trouble looks in, asks
should I stay or should I go?
Staying it is.

Trouble announces its arrival
at the worst moment possible.
I'm here with you now,
trouble smirks.

Not what you want?
Not what you long for?
Not what you deserve?
No matter.

I'm here now,
and there's no going back.
There's only your hope that
I won't persevere.

INVISIBLE

The first time it happened, I didn't really think anything of it. I'd come into work early that Monday morning to get things organized before the week started. Bob, our only salesman, came in a few minutes after I arrived.

"Hey! I stopped in Friday before closing time to see you. Thought you might want to stop off for a drink before going home. Left early, huh?" He didn't look at me when he said this. Bob knew I never left early on Fridays. My life was routine and dry as chalk. I was never in a hurry to go home to Fred and another long weekend of baseball, NASCAR, and Budweiser.

"No," I answered, taking notice of his newly trimmed hair. Was he wearing a new brown sports coat? Bob seemed to be coming out of the slump he'd been in since his wife Jeanette's sudden death last month. "I was here, Bob. You know I never leave early."

"Well, it was just after four. I waited until after five when everyone else left." Bob looked at me strangely. "Maybe you were in the bathroom? Running copies? Something?"

53

"I was right here, Bob. Right here at my desk where I am every Friday afternoon." My voice sounded harsh. I smiled in an attempt to soften what I'd just said. I liked Bob. He was a good salesman and a nice man. Right then the phone rang, and even though it wasn't yet eight, I answered. Might be that big commission that put us ahead for the year. I didn't want to miss it if it was.

Well, of course, it wasn't. Actually it was a wrong number, and by the time I looked at the space in front of my desk where Bob had just been standing, he was gone. I was surprised to find myself thinking about what it might have been like, having a drink with him, after work, on a Friday. Not hurrying home to Fred and the television.

I worked in a small engineering office, had been there twenty years. Life was pretty humdrum since both the kids were grown. They'd moved out-of-state, seeking a better life than what they'd seen Fred and me live. Oh, they still called, every Sunday, regular as clockwork. Daryl in the morning, Darlene in the afternoon. Short calls. "Hi Mom. How's Dad? How's the office?" That sort of thing. Neither had married so there were no grandkids to brighten the holidays, and most years they spent Christmas with friends rather than flying down to see Fred and me.

The next two weeks were uneventful. Then it happened again. This time it was my boss, Mr. Harper, bursting in through the door, flustered. "Where the hell were you? I needed your help and you weren't here." He leaned over my desk and yelled, "Where the hell were you?" Before I could answer, he'd stormed into his office and slammed the door.

At first I didn't know what to think. I didn't even leave my desk to go to the bathroom or take a break, unless it was my lunch hour. Most days I even ate lunch at the picnic table outside the back door, the table where customers sometimes smoked while waiting to see Mr. Harper.

I spoke to the closed office door. "Mr. Harper? Are you okay?" It'd been unseasonably hot for April. I thought maybe he'd gotten too much sun or something. He could be having heat stroke, and I tried to remember what to do. Was it water? Whiskey? Wait and hope it would pass on its own?

"Deficient!" Mr. Harper yelled at me from behind the closed door. "Your performance is deficient!"

I sat at my desk, stared at the clock as though the answer to my confusion would appear with the next tick. Just fifteen minutes until my lunch break when I could sit outside and listen to the mockingbird that always seemed to be singing his heart out perched on the utility pole at the corner of the property. I wondered if anyone else heard his beautiful songs.

Then two days later on Friday afternoon, Bob came in and looked at me strangely. "Stopped by before lunch today, thought I might buy *you* lunch." He continued to stare. I ran my hand through my shaggy hair, pulled the worn cardigan closer.

I was always cold in the office. I left the sweater on the back of my chair so it'd be there when I needed it. I couldn't remember how long I'd had that sweater. Maybe I should replace it with something newer. I had clothes hanging in my closet that I never wore, things the kids sent for Christmas and my birthday. I could bring in something else from home.

"So where were you?" Bob interrupted my clothing reverie. "Have an appointment or something?"

"I was right here, Bob. You know I never leave early for lunch. Mr. Harper counts on me to be here."

"Your desk was empty," Bob looked put out about something. I wondered if he really was getting over his wife's death. It had been so sudden, and I knew he'd had some problems adjusting.

"You must be mistaken, Bob. I was right here." My heart skipped a beat at being so forceful. I liked Bob, really did like him. Was that another new sports coat he was wearing? And new shoes?

"Well, I sure didn't see you. Are you fooling around or something? Got a new man in your life?"

I didn't like the sudden menace I heard in his voice, so personal, so...so inquisitive, so unlike Bob. I picked up a stack of papers and walked into the next room to the copier, busied myself running blank copies until he finally left. I put the clean, still-warm white paper back in the tray and returned to my desk.

Well, next thing I know it's Sunday night and my son called. "Hi Mom? Been out? I called earlier and you didn't answer." We both knew Fred hadn't answered the phone since he retired last year. "Done with that," he said and that was the end of his talking on the phone.

"I was here, son, all morning, waiting for your call. Are you sure...." I trailed off not knowing what else to say.

By the first of May, everyone was mad at me for not being there when they called or when they wanted something or needed some mail dropped off at the post office on my way home. Even Fred complained that I wasn't there to fix his dinner when he wanted it. Mr. Harper said if this continued, he was going to advertise my position in the newspaper, and I'd be expected to train my replacement. He needed someone he could depend on.

The next day I stopped by the walk-in clinic I passed on my way home. Maybe I needed some medication. I wasn't used to everybody being angry with me all the time. I needed something to calm my nerves. I couldn't go on like this.

I walked through the outside door, stepped into the vestibule. A young mother, carrying a screaming baby, pushed open the door and rushed by, nearly knocking me down. I blinked in sympathy. She was so upset she didn't even see me. That's what it's like with your first one, I remembered. Nothing else exists when the baby's screaming like that.

I waited for her to finish with the receptionist, waited until she'd been taken back to an examining room, before I walked closer. The young blonde behind the glass window didn't look up. I shifted my weight, foot to foot, thinking the movement would catch her attention.

It didn't.

I cleared my throat. Ahem. I knew that would get her attention. There was no one else in the waiting room, no TV blaring, no radio. Just the sound of me clearing my throat.

She didn't move.

I reached up and tapped a fingernail against the glass, annoyed now at being ignored. She turned and walked from the small office, into the hallway. Didn't look my way.

I took a chair in the empty waiting room. I knew I was getting older, not as attractive as I once was. Everyone knows when a woman reaches a certain age, she becomes invisible. At least that's what my best friend Carol had told me. She was angry when it started happening to her. I'd never really believed it, but I was starting to wonder if she wasn't right.

Suddenly I needed to use the rest room, spotted the door over near the corner, opposite the entryway. I'd just freshen up a bit, then wait until the receptionist returned. I'd get her attention this time.

I walked into the small closet of a bathroom, wondered what germs lurked there, how many days since anyone had cleaned the place. The young blonde who hadn't seen me didn't look like she'd clean the restrooms each day like I'd done at the office the past twenty years.

I flipped on the light, stared into the white framed mirror above the white porcelain sink.

I saw nothing. No one looked back at me.

My heart fluttered. I placed my left hand on my chest, the one with my wedding ring, the small gold band Fred had given me on our wedding day, thirty-five years ago. I looked again at the mirror, searched for the small gold posts in my ears, the ones Fred had given me on our first anniversary. The only earrings I'd worn since that day.

No one looked back.

I looked down at the wedding band, fourth finger on my wrinkled left hand. Nothing there. I watched in horror as my hand slowly disappeared.

I looked again at the empty mirror. Lifted my right hand to touch my face.

Nothing.

Suddenly I understood. I'd disappeared, even from myself. I was gone. Undetectable. Indistinguishable. Invisible.

I wondered if anyone would miss me.

The next morning when the young, blonde medical assistant came in early to clean the waiting room rest room, she found two small gold stud earrings and a plain gold wedding band on the floor. She slipped them in her pocket thinking someone would call looking for them later in the day. She put away her cleaning supplies, and took her place behind the sliding glass window that separated her from the clinic waiting room.

By the time the first patient walked through the door, coughing and sneezing, she'd forgotten all about the earrings and the gold wedding band in her pocket.

CONVERSATIONS

My head is full of people,
but they don't live in my house.
Some I've known,
others are strangers.

Some are friends,
many are not.
They talk to me,
constantly

whispering, mumbling, shouting.
They have incessant voices.
Sometimes they're supportive,
sometimes they manipulate me.

If I had a bigger house,
I'd give them all rooms
to occupy.
And phones

so they could talk to each other.

My number would be unlisted.

HAPPY HOUR

Dora looked across the round table top littered with small white plates and half-filled wine glasses. "Are you still dating Dean?"

"Ah, Dean, no, not dating, but I talk to him more now than I did in the nine months before we broke up. Now he's seeing Miss Fatal Attraction. Yeah, I threw him out about nine months ago. He didn't come home for three nights and when he did, I said, 'Dean, this just isn't the kind of relationship I wanted. Marriage, you remember the M word?'" Del leans forward as she says this and her face flushes bright red.

Fern and Iris make eye contact across the littered table. Dora hears their silent 'You had to ask, didn't you?' as they both glare silently at her. Too late to back out now though.

"Yes, I remember when you said you were going to marry him." Dora slides back in her chair.

"Well, he weaseled out of that one, he did. Met Miss Fatal Attraction, he did. We're all in the Praise Choir at church." Del–short for Delilah–stops here, smiles sweetly, makes eye contact with Dora, Iris and

61

Fern, one at a time, as if bowing to the congregation. Dora pictures the three of them –Del, Dean, and Miss Fatal Attraction–singing sweetly together in the Praise Choir.

Del continues, "And is she a piece of work? Tall, thin, had a hooter job, looks like tits on a stick. They're so big she can't hardly stand up straight." She laughs. "Musta been really small before that boob job. We'd already talked to the preacher about the vows, remember?"

Del turns toward Fern and Iris. "Remember, you were going to help me with the reception?"

Before either can reply, Del slaps one hand to the table. "Yep, Miss Fatal Attraction, that one. Erased his hard drive, deleted all his cell phone numbers."

"Erased his hard drive?" Dora croaks. "Now that's nasty."

"I been helping him get it back. It's taken hours. Miss Fatal Attraction knew what she was doing, I'll say that."

Iris, Fern and Dora are hooked now, waiting to hear the rest of the details.

Del was just getting wound up. "Four years, I can't believe it, I spent four years on that man, but the Good Lord has other plans for me, I just know he does. He just has too. That's what the Preacher says, 'Now Delilah, honey, you know the good Lord don't lead you nowhere he won't get you out of. When the Lord closes a door, well then, he'll just open a window for you to jump through.'"

Dora pictures the Lord slamming the door in Del's face, Dean standing on the other side kissing Miss Fatal Attraction tits on a stick, and giving Del a window with bars on it. By the time that image fades, Del is on to something else.

"She came up to me last week after Praise practice, says, 'Now, I don't want no trouble.' I say, 'No trouble, honey, you can have him, there's not going to be trouble.' She looks me up and down and asks, 'How old are you?' I smile, stand straight up and say, '48.' 'Forty-eight? You're kidding me, I thought you were the same age as Dean, 36. My, well, I'd never guess. You look real good for a woman your age.' 'A woman my age.'" Del snorts. "Can you believe it. Let's see what those fake tits will look like hanging on that skinny body when she's a woman my age." Del rolls her eyes and moves on.

"Course Bryce had to call him when he looked for a new truck. Dean knows more about engines than anyone else, and Bryce knows nothing. Dean was real good about it too. They bought a new Dodge Ram, four-passenger doors, dual exhausts, 4-wheel drive, cargo management system, all the bells and whistles."

Bryce is Del's nineteen year old son with a supposedly mild case of cerebral palsy. Limps slightly when he walks. According to Del, it doesn't slow him down much and the life expectancy has improved from the 30 short years it was when Bryce was born, thanks to modern medicine and good insurance coverage.

"Bryce moved back home, did I tell ya? We've been on this new diet. Yeah, it's great, he does the yard now that Dean's gone, cleans the kitchen every night after dinner. Works out with my weights in the morning before work, looks great." Another of those winning smiles from the proud mom. "He's back at Publix so he does all the shopping. I'm so proud of him."

This glowing smile is interrupted by a cell phone blaring a brassy rendition of Amazing Grace. "Oh, that's Dean now. Hi, honey."

Honey? Fern, Iris, and Dora look at one another. Iris winks.

"Oh sure, honey, I'm just leaving. I'll be home in an hour. You and Bryce are eating fried chicken from

Publix? Well, save me some, I know how you big boys eat...and I'm hungry." Del slides the nearly empty plate of potato skins toward the middle of the table. "Okay, sweetie, see you soon."

"Well, whadda you know, he's at the house with Bryce. They went out looking for chrome wheels today. The Dodge came with factory wheels and Dean's been telling Bryce, no self-respecting man would be seen around town with those wheels. Gotta have chrome wheels." Another big smile.

"It's been so good to see ya'll. We've got to do this again soon. And don't you worry, I'm done with Dean. I know the good Lord has something better planned for me, just like Preacher says. And I put all my faith in the Lord, always have, you ladies know that. Look at everything He brung me through so far...well, gotta run. My boys are waitin'."

UNINVITED GUESTS

Hello! Hello! Hello!

I'm so full of myself
I can barely see you there.

Can you come closer?
I'm not sure you can hear me
as well as I'd like you to.

Did I tell you the whole
world knows who I am and
where I've been and what I've done?

Oh? You haven't heard of me?
Let me fill you in.
Just a brief bio.

I know you'll find me fascinating.

BOBBIE SUE AND BUBBA

Bobbie Sue and Bubba met at the No Tell Motel just across the county line at eleven o'clock every Wednesday for the past nine years. Unless, of course, Wednesday was Christmas or some other family holiday, then Bubba stayed home with his wife, Mary Jane, and their three kids, two boys and a girl.

It all started after Bobbie Sue's husband, Reynard, came home from Iraq not quite the man he was when he went in. Bubba'd stopped by Bobbie Sue's beauty salon, Hair of Glory, to express his heart-felt sympathy. Bubba and Bobbie Sue fooled around some in high school, mostly after football games, but he married Benny Gardner's daughter and moved comfortably into her family's insurance business, as he'd always known he would.

He liked Bobbie Sue, liked her a lot, and he was ever so thankful it hadn't been his legs blown off, just above the knees. So he did the Christian thing. He stepped in to help. And he'd helped as best he could just about every Wednesday for the past nine years. He always tucked a hundred dollar bill in Bobbie Sue's handbag when she was in the bathroom freshening up,

67

after. She never mentioned it and neither did he. Just another part of their unspoken agreement, but over the years the money had come in handy. Reynard had a hard time keeping a job. Hair of Glory was a successful salon, but even successful businesses have thin times.

Today it was past eleven thirty and Bubba still hadn't shown. Bobbie Sue ate her half of the pizza and eyed Bubba's half. She shook her head no and finished her sweet tea.

She was in the bathroom when she heard the knock. She unbuttoned the top two buttons on her blouse, checked her lipstick, and opened the door.

Mary Jane stood outside, hands on her hips, looking much like she had in high school. "Bubba ain't coming this week, Bobbie Sue. In fact, he ain't ever meetin' you here again." Mary Jane rubbed her hands together and said, "Well, you gonna invite me in or what?" She pushed through the door into the shabby room. "It ain't like this is a surprise to either of us, now is it." She sat carefully on the wooden chair next to the unruffled bed. She looked at the pizza box, then at Bobbie Sue. "May I?"

Bobbie Sue nodded. Mary Jane ate a slice of pizza without speaking. "Missed breakfast." She patted her lips with a paper napkin, then looked at Bobbie Sue. "Damn. You don't know, do you?"

"What are you talking about, Mary Jane?"

"Bubba's gone. The office was surrounded when he arrived this morning. IRS. The Feds. They were everywhere. I haven't seen so many black suits and crew cuts since Uncle Jack's funeral." She paused and smiled. "You were there, in the back. I saw ya." Mary Jane opened the pizza box, then closed it again.

"You're Miss Wednesday, Bobbie Sue. Don't think you're so damn special, honey. There's a Miss Monday and a Miss Friday too, only none of them girls lasted as long as you."

"Mary Jane..." Bobbie Sue started to speak but thought better of it.

"It's okay, honey. I've known for a long time what Bubba's been up to. Cheatin' with his Monday, Wednesday, and Friday girls. And cheatin' in the business too. I've planned for this day. The kids and I are going to be fine. Just fine. I've gotten my insurance licenses and once all this brouhaha blows over, I'll reopen and we'll all be able to move on."

Bobbie Sue nodded. "I'm sorry, Mary Jane. Really sorry. You don't deserve this."

Mary Jane removed a large brown envelope from her purse. "And you deserve better than Reynard, honey. We're pretty much in the same boat." She handed the envelope to Bobbie Sue. "That's from Bubba. He gave it to me this morning, just before...." She blinked a few times before continuing. "I think there's a letter in there, too. And cash, honey, lots of cash."

Bobbie Sue looked at the envelope then shook her head. "I can't..."

"Just take it, honey. You deserve it, putting up with Bubba all these years. We both coulda done better, don't you know."

"But...." Bobbie Sue stopped trying to protest when Mary Jane leaned in and hugged her close.

"The Feds don't know about this, Bobbie Sue. You and me and Bubba are the only ones who know. He wants you to have it, so take it. He gave it to me this morning to give to you, before they took him away. No one's the wiser, and God knows, I'll bet you can use it."

Bobbie Sue opened the large manila envelope, saw a folded piece of paper and several rubber-banded packets of hundred dollar bills.

A smile broke across her face as she looked back at Mary Jane. "You're a good woman, and I wish you the best. Anytime you want a new do, honey, just stop by the shop, and I'll fix you right up for the professional world. Hair, make-up, the works." She winked. "On the house."

"Put me down for next Wednesday, eleven o'clock, Bobbie Sue. I think you have an opening and God knows, we have lots of catching up to do." In high school both girls had been junior varsity cheerleaders.

Bobbie Sue watched Mary Jane's pearl white Cadillac Escalade pull out from the motel parking lot. She patted the envelope and resisted the urge to count the hundred dollar bills inside. *Later. I can do that later. Reynard's always down at the bar anyway. It'll give me something to do.*

She took one last look at the worn room, walked out to her car, and wondered if the maid would eat the remaining pizza. She'd go back to Hair of Glory and have time to put the envelope in the wall safe behind Reynard's picture hanging in her office before her afternoon appointments. *Maybe it's time to take that ugly mug of his down and move on, like Mary Jane.*

She recognized Hank, the motel manager, standing outside the office door, leering as she drove away. She powered down her window. "We won't need the room next week, Hank. Won't need it ever again. You can read all about it in tomorrow's Gazette." She gave him her best smile, pulled back into the parking space outside the room, removed one of the hundred dollar bills from the envelope, dashed in and tucked the bill under the pizza box for the maid to find.

As she pulled away from the motel, Bobbie Sue heard her old Sunday School teacher's voice in her head. "When your good fortune increases, pay it forward and set another place at the table."

She and Bubba'd sat through many Sunday mornings at the small church where his daddy taught Sunday School. "All the justice don't happen at the courthouse," he often told them.

She took a last look at the seedy motel and smiled. *Indeed it don't.*

HAPPINESS

Thinking about happiness—
it shouldn't be so hard.
We're meant to be happy after all.
Why else would we be here?

Countless self-help books and articles,
counseling, workshops, in-services.
Analyzing, dissecting, disassembling, releasing.
Oh God, yes, releasing it all.

Then one day it happens.
Contentment.
A couple of years later
wandering alone in the yard,

realization.
Happiness.
This is what happiness is,
so simple, so natural, so easy.

CROSSROADS

The first sound Marcella heard each morning was the coughing and sputtering of the old rusted pickup truck leaving the complex. That sound told her it was time to crawl from under the pile of knitted afghans and fix her morning bowl of Cheerios which she ate standing alone at the small kitchen window watching the squirrels outside run from tree to tree.

Once her mama Lorraine got up and began her day, Marcella delivered packages to people in the complex. Small brown paper wrapped packages that they took from her, always placing a twenty dollar bill in her hand when they did. She dutifully stuffed the bill in her pocket, walked straight back to her apartment, handed the bill to Lorraine and watched as she stuffed the bills in the small colorful zippered bag purchased at a local craft fair the summer before.

Marcella knew where her mama kept the little black spiral-bound notebook she marked in each time she returned with a twenty stuffed in her pocket. She knew where the Mason jar was stored, the Mason jar where every tenth bill from her trips was placed. Mama called it the tithing jar. "Every tenth one, Marcella. Every tenth one goes in the tithing jar 'cause I know the Lord has a better place for us. It's for the Lord's plan, Marcella. The Bible says to tithe, so we tithin'."

Marcella knew how to count to one hundred, how to make change for twenties from bills as large as a hundred. She knew how to wrap the small packages she delivered to nearly every unit in the fenced apartment complex where she and her mother lived.

Once a week they left the complex when the big bus with a bright blue cat painted on the side picked them up and carried them down to the Winn Dixie where they traded the other pieces of paper Mama got for food. Mama always bought lots of cheese, fatty bacon, grits, sometimes shrimp, but mostly she bought Cheerios in big boxes and two percent milk, always brought it home in brown paper bags.

Marcella knew nearly everyone in her complex. Some were nice, others never even looked at her when she knocked on their doors. They just grabbed the small wrapped package and shoved a twenty in her face. Most of them never mentioned her crossed eyes, but the fat one always did. "Get on outta here, you cross-eyed little brat." Said the same thing each time Marcella delivered her package.

Her favorite was the dark man who lived in the back, closest to the dumpster, the man who mowed the scraggly yard and did odd jobs around the complex after he returned from work each day. He called her Angel Eyes and sometimes gave her bubble gum when she walked by his apartment delivering a package to someone else, never to him. She called him Blue.

Every Friday night Uncle Dominic came with his large black duffle. He always brought her a half-eaten bag of Fritos and let her eat the rest of them all by herself. Mama always had a big pot of cabbage steaming on the stove the night Uncle Dominic came, so the whole house smelled kinda bad, but Mama said she needed to make that 'cause what Dominic brought in his black duffle smelled even worse.

Marcella didn't think it did, but she never argued with Mama. Always went to her room and stayed there eating Fritos until Uncle Dominic left and Mama told her she could come out and start wrapping the little baggies in the paper cut from the brown Winn Dixie bags. Sometimes this took a long time, but Marcella never complained, just sat and wrapped and taped while Mama talked on the phone.

Those nights she was busy long after dark delivering small packages all over the complex. Mama kept the cabbage simmering on the stove until she was done and then threw the smelly stuff in the garbage which she had Marcella take down to the dumpster. Sometimes she saw the Blue man and he would wave at her. She'd wave back and run as fast as she could back to her own apartment.

At the end of each week, Lorraine would take out the Mason jar stuffed with twenty dollar bills and have Marcella count them. "It's our escape money, honey," she'd smile when the counting was finished. "When we get enough money, we're outta here. Your Aunt Marcella, the one I named you after, lives in Georgia in her own house. With a yard. There's a school nearby where you can go and another school where I can study cosmetology and learn to be a beautician like I always wanted. What do you think of that?"

Marcella would smile, nod, and hug her mama. It was the same every week. She never asked how much money would be enough, but just kept delivering the brown paper bag wrapped packages to nearly every door in the complex.

Marcella had done this for as long as she could remember. She didn't mind the work, only a couple of people were mean to her, the rest just smiled happily when she handed them their package.

Uncle Dominic visited each week on Friday night. He never stayed long, just long enough to transact business, give Lorraine a quick kiss and be gone. He hated the smell of boiling cabbage, said it clung to his clothes.

But this Friday night Uncle Dominic didn't show up at his normal time. It was well past midnight when he started banging on the flimsy door, waking Lorraine and Marcella and neighbors all around the apartment.

As soon as Lorraine opened the door, Uncle Dominic yelled louder, starting kicking the furniture and waving the pistol he always carried with him. Lorraine started screaming, "Are you crazy? Put that gun away!"

Marcella stood clinging to Lorraine' long red nightgown and didn't resist when Lorraine shoved her into her bedroom and slammed the door.

"Put that gun away! The neighbors will call the police … is that what you want, Dominic, you want the police to come?"

Marcella crawled under the shiny red coverlet covering her mother's bed and pulled the pillow over her head, but she could still hear the screaming. First Lorraine screaming to put the gun away, then Uncle Dominic yelling "Shut up, bitch. Just shut the fuck up."

At the sound of the gun shots, Marcella wet her pants, something she hadn't done for a over a year now. She wanted to get up and change her clothes, change the sheets, but the gun shots kept her anchored under the pillow, hands covering her ears, breath ragged. She figured her mama would understand this one time.

Uncle Dominic shot until the gun was empty, placed six round holes in the white ceiling tile. Lorraine screamed and screamed until he hit her in the face and she shut up. "Where's that fucking jar, bitch? I need that goddamn jar o' yours. Where the fuck is it?"

Lorraine didn't even look at the small noisy refrigerator in the corner of the kitchen, willed herself not to even look in that direction. Dominic pulled the cushions from the worn sofa, kicked the battered coffee table across the room, swept some dishes from the cupboard, but Lorraine didn't look up, just sat down on the floor and kept her hands over her face. She could already feel the bruises forming.

The neighbors called the police who arrived forty-five minutes later, long after Dominic was gone. He'd emptied the revolver into the ceiling, hit Lorraine in the face several times, and trashed their tired living room. The complex was not a favorite stop for the local police and by the time they arrived Dominic had done his damage and was gone, taking his unemptied duffle bag with him. A formal report was not filed.

It was dawn before Lorraine let Marcella out of her room. "Go get Blue, Marcella, ask him to come over here."

Marcella ran to Blue's apartment, tapped on the door until he finally answered, rubbing sleep from his eyes. He said nothing, but pulled on his t-shirt and he followed her home.

"I've got money, Blue." Lorraine pleaded. "I can pay you to take me to my sister's in Georgia."

Blue took a step back, gazed at the bullet-riddled ceiling, at the bruises on Lorraine' face, at the overturned furniture, finally at Marcella who stood behind her mother, eyes wide and sucking her thumb.

"Well, I reckon," Blue spoke softly. "Pack your stuff and be ready in an hour. I'll go borrow my brother's truck and we'll go soon as I get back." He shut the splintered front door behind him.

True to his word, Blue returned in a hour in an older black Dodge pickup, stowed their meager belongings stuffed in black plastic garbage bags in the bed of the truck, used bungee cords to tie them down and, stood by the driver's side door waiting patiently until they were both inside.

Marcella sat between Lorraine and Blue on the wide bench seat. Lorraine didn't look back, but leaned against the door and sobbed, loud noisy snotty sobs that lasted so long Marcella wondered if she would ever stop crying. Finally, Blue put a CD of some old blues music in the player. Lulled by the raspy voice on the tape, Lorraine finally sobbed herself to sleep.

A few more miles rolled away before Blue spoke for the first time since they'd been on the road. "That there is Robert Johnson you're listening too. He's a famous old bluesman singing the Delta blues."

Marcella relaxed against Blue's strong arm. "Delta?"

"The Mississippi Delta, child. That song you're hearing is 'Crossroads.' That's where you and your mama are right now, at a crossroads."

Marsella leaned into Blue, wondering just what he meant.

"Crossroads?" she asked.

"It's a place where a decision has to be made. You can go this way or you can go that way, but you got to choose one over the other."

The gravelly voice on the CD sang, "I went down to the crossroads, fell down on my knees."

Blue continued. "Your mama went down on her knees when she sent you to get me. She's at a crossroads, you see. You at a crossroads too."

"You mean…leaving here and going to see Aunt Marcella in Georgia?"

"That's exactly what I mean, child. Your mama made a choice, a good choice when she sent you to get me and axed me to take you to Georgia."

"Will things be better there, Blue? Will things be better for us?"

"The good Lord willing, Marcella, things are going to be a whole lot better for you and your mama."

"I hope so, Blue. I really hope so. Uncle Dominic hurt Mama bad."

"He ain't your uncle, child. He's ain't no relation to you at all. He's the devil's pawn and no relation to you or your mama, you hear me. Don't believe that ever again." Blue shifted his right arm from the steering wheel and drew Marcella closer to him. "The good Lord come for you this day and got me to drive you and your mama to Georgia. I'll be praying for you, Marcella. For you and your mama and your Aunt Marcella too. Things is going to change for you, girl. You be going to school. Your mama got enough money saved in that Mason jar so she can go to school too. Can learn that hair dressing and get a real job. No more pushing dope and hiding away from what's good and right. You hear me, Marcella? That's what the good Lord's got in store for you.

"You gonna have to be strong now, Marcella. No more running packages door to door, no matter if your mama axes you to or not. You gonna go to school, you gonna learn things to help you in this world. Lorraine is gonna go to school too, you got to make sure of that, you hear me?"

Marcella nodded yes. "I hear you, Blue. And thanks for helping us. I thought Uncle Dominic...Dominic was gonna kill Mama and then where would I be?" Her shoulders began to shake and she slumped into the seat, drew herself tighter against Blue.

"It's okay, child. You done taken the right turn at that crossroads. Remember that. You done made the right choice and you're gonna continue on down that road to a better place. It's like the man says in another song, 'I once was lost, and now I'm found, was blind but now I see.' You understand what that means, Marcella? You seeing right, now. You gonna work hard and see what's good in life."

81

Marcella took her thumb from her mouth and sat up straighter. "Yessir, Blue, I understand what you're saying. 'I once was lost and now I'm found, was blind and now I see.' And so will Mama, Blue. Now Mama will see too."

AS SEEN ON TV

I'm dysfunctional – you can be too. Just follow these 26 easy steps and see how easy it is. You can annoy your friends and family in less than a month. Just do one easy step a day, and soon you'll be annoying not just some, but all of your friends and family. We guarantee it or your money back. But wait! Order now and you will receive not one, not two, but three copies of this laminated list of easy behaviors to cultivate. Carry it in your purse or wallet. Soon you'll be as dysfunctional as the rest of the world.

ABCs of Dysfunction

Aberrant
Braggart
Cantankerous
Defiant
Envious
Frustrating
Greedy
Helpless
Idiotic
Joyless
Know-nothing

Licentious
Masochistic
Narcissistic
Obnoxious
Psychotic
Quarrelsome
Rude
Secretive
Tactless
Unfeeling
Vacant
Wastrel
Xenophobic
Yellow
Zealous

See how easy it is? You can run with the Big Boys when you too are a world-class rat bastard. It takes less than a month. Money-back guarantee if you're not completely satisfied.

(See fine print on back for more details.)

DEAD ED

Cyn wasn't fat, she was just fluffy, spent too many long hours doing just what she was doing now. Sitting in a bar drinking scotch and waters. Too few long walks on the beach.

She wasn't old either, just a bit over the top of prime. That is if you could think of a good ten to fifteen years as being a bit over the top of prime.

The Blue Moon was her hangout these days. Some days she was good for business, some days not so much. Some days she sat by herself, nursing one scotch after another, smoking one Virginia Slims menthol cigarette after another, staring out at unceasing waves coming in from the Atlantic.

Cyn had a lot of friends, not all were men. Some were women like her, sidetracked somewhere along the way by a couple of kids and a divorce. She'd always enjoyed life, never spent much time looking past tomorrow. Having fun came easy to her, always had.

But today was not a good day, not a good day at all. It was the anniversary of Ed's death, the fifth anniversary to be exact. Her third husband, Ed—Dead Ed as she'd called him since his untimely demise—was the least favorite of her three husbands. Today his spirit had descended on her with both heavy feet. The day hadn't been pretty so far, and the sun was still high in the faded blue sky.

After three scotch and waters, she lost count. Norm the bartender set another in front of her, took the empty, and kept them coming. It didn't matter from where.

The small beachside bar was starting to fill, mostly sunburned tourists wandering in. The memory of Ed's death pushed their noise away. All she could hear was his breathing, shallow and harsh, a memory from that last night.

"I'll have what she's having," A tanned man wearing a heavy gold necklace, a muscle shirt, and swim trunks had taken the seat next to her. He turned to Cyn, flashed a smile of well-kept dental work, and extended his hand. "I'm Ed. And you, lovely lady, are?"

"Cyn, short for Cynthia."

"Well, nice to meet ya, Cyn, short for Cynthia." Another flash of the million dollar smile. "Bring one for Cyn," Ed said when Norm placed his glass on the bar.

Cyn struggled to pull herself from the past, taking in the three diamond rings adorning manicured fingers, the heavy gold bracelet on his right hand, matching the heavy gold chain around his neck. The diamond encrusted gold Rolex. No wedding ring, she was quick to notice. This one might be interesting.

The afternoon slowly faded into evening. Ed, it turned out, was the general manager of the local Toyota dealership, spending a rare day off working on his tan. She could already smell the money.

Scotch continued to flow and after a shared snack of greasy wings with blue cheese dressing and an order of fried mushrooms, Ed invited Cyn to join him at his condo. She could leave her car here, he'd drive, and drop her back by the Blue Moon when he went into the city to work tomorrow.

She agreed. Ed draped one arm across her shoulders as they stumbled more than walked to the parking lot. The aged parking lot guard watched them struggle to enter the low-slung Nissan 370Z Roadster, shaking his head. Ned had seen it all before. He was still shaking his head as the Z car slowly and erratically backed from the parking lot onto the narrow street and sped away.

A few short miles down the road, Ed swiped his card in the magnetic reader of the large gated condo complex, pulled into a spot facing a two story building. "Here we are, princess."

Ed managed to stumble to the passenger side door and pull Cyn from the bucket seat. "Not much farther now, princess." Ed draped his arm around Cyn's shoulder and together they managed to walk up the flight of stairs to Ed's second story unit. He struggled with the lock and after a couple of tries opened the door and switched on the light. "Here we are, princess. Home sweet home."

Cyn shrugged his alarmingly heavy arm off her shoulders and walked through the sterile, masculine, chrome and black leather living room to the sliding glass doors overlooking the Atlantic. "Quite a view," she managed to say before returning to the black Barcalounger and flopping into it.

Ed walked to the bar and poured them both a large crystal tumbler of Chevis. "Here's to ya, princess." He handed her a tumbler, took a large swig from his and crumpled face down on the floor.

"Damn," Cyn spoke out loud. "Déjà vu all over again," she mumbled before taking a small sip of the Chevis. "Mmmm, so much better that the well stuff at the Blue Moon." She sat back in the chair, closed her eyes, and passed out.

The clock over the fireplace showed three thirty. It took a few seconds to realize where she was. Ed was still crumpled on the floor where he had fallen. Didn't look like he'd moved.

Cyn switched on the table lamp next to the lounger, squinted away from the bright light. She pushed herself out of the chair and slowly walked around the apartment, occasionally looking over to where Ed was lying unmoving on the floor.

Cyn found Ed's bedroom, switched on the light and stood in the doorway. Quite a change from the rest of the immaculate condo. More black lacquered furniture, but clothes were strewn everywhere, on the bed, on the floor, covering the two occasional chairs facing the ocean, draped over the treadmill. Ugh. Dirty underwear, socks, t-shirts. Swim trunks covered the towel bars in the bathroom, flip flops on the floor. What was he thinking inviting her over to this mess?

She spotted a large jewelry armoire on the littered dresser, walked to it, started pulling open drawers, each filled with heavy gold chains, bracelets, cuff links, tie tacks. One drawer was completely filled with diamond rings. Hmmmm. She turned and walked back to the living room. Ed was still on the floor. She wondered if he was okay, but didn't choose to check, instead walked back to the armoire. Would he miss any of this stuff if it somehow disappeared?

A gurgling sound roused her from her thoughts. It sounded just like third husband Dead Ed the night he died. She walked over to the body. At least he was still breathing, but that gurgling sound was making her skin crawl. She wondered if she should call for help, decided to walk to the bathroom and look in the mirror.

A quick glance told her the answer she sought. She couldn't greet visitors looking like this. Her mascara was streaked, her hair stuck out at odd angles. She decided to pee, thought of looking for a washcloth for her face, then decided that would leave more evidence than she wanted.

"Evidence?" A voice in her head asked. "You're worried about evidence?"

The idea clarified in her mind. No one knew she was there…well there was that old fart, Ned, the cranky parking lot guard at Blue Moon, but he'd seen her leave with several men over the summer so she didn't know if he'd even remember who she left with tonight. She'd never seen Ed in the Blue Moon before which indicated he wasn't a regular.

She had fourteen dollars in her purse and no food in the fridge of the small travel trailer she used during the summer. And that bastard, Dead Ed, had left her nothing. Not one penny. She'd even had to pay for his cremation expenses. Son of a bitch. She tried to remember what this Ed looked like, decided he looked like Dead Ed. At least this one had some money. All that jewelry, the car, this condo.

It was time for some compensation, some Ed compensation. She walked back to the bedroom, went through the armoire one drawer at a time, wrapping a wrinkled handkerchief over her fingers. No use leaving any more prints.

She decided to remove only one thing from each drawer. She counted fourteen small drawers and two larger ones. She quickly chose one item from each and stuffed them down her bra. The bottom drawer was full of watches. Three Rolex, two Tag Heuers. My goodness Ed had a lot of jewelry.

She fastened one watch on each wrist and decided it was time to skedaddle. But how would she get back to her car? She dismissed calling for a cab, no need to attract any more attention. She checked the clock over the bar. Four fifteen, still an hour or so before sunrise. Maybe she would just drive herself back to the Blue

Moon in Ed's car. Let him worry about it. Damn Eds anyway. She'd never liked that name.

She found the keys in an ornate bowl on the table inside the front door. Checked to see that Ed was still breathing, let herself out of the apartment, locked it, used the handkerchief to wipe any prints from the knob, and walked down to the silver Z. "Nice ride," she thought. "Wonder why he's not driving a Toyota."

The next day she slept well into the afternoon, leaving the small trailer only to take a long walk on the beach. She finished the food from several take-out boxes in the small fridge and fell asleep shortly after sunset.

She awoke early the next morning, showered, dressed, and walked over to her favorite breakfast place. She chose a table facing the ocean, picked up a newspaper from the unused chair next to her. Flipped through to find the front section. She prided herself on keeping up with current events.

A large headline on the third page caught her attention. "Sunshine Toyota General Manager Found Dead in Condo." *Oh my god!* She quickly skimmed the article. "Discovered by a salesman the dealership sent over after he didn't show up for work yesterday morning. Found dead on the living room floor. A blood toxicology report had been ordered, but foul play was not suspected. Ed Magruder was recently divorced. Ralph Oder, the owner of the Toyota dealership, was quoted as saying, 'Ed just hadn't been himself these days. He just couldn't get over losing his wife and kids.'"

Naomi the waitress, looking harried, walked over to Cyn's table just as she folded the newspaper and placed it in her purse. "Coffee, honey?" she asked.

A bright smile crossed Cyn's make-up free face. "Yes. And a large shrimp and grits with andouille sausage. And a Bloody Mary, lots of garnish. Today is a damned special day."

In her mind she was already designing the diamond necklace she would have made from several of Ed's rings. It would be a real mankiller.

HELP!

Help me if you can,
I'm feeling FINE!
I haven't even been into the wine.

No weeds destroy the symmetry of my yard.
The fridge is full, the freezer's packed,
even the toads are growing.

Friends call, activities mark the calendar.
Facebook tells me I'm alive and well in cyberworld,
hearing from old relatives and former classmates.

There's money in my pocket,
some left over in the checkbook.
The bills are all paid.

Not a worry in the world.
Not a care in my heart.
My soul is untroubled.

And I don't know what to do with myself.

Help me if you can.
I'm feeling FINE!
JUST FINE!

DRUM BEAT

"Look at the smoke hanging in the air."

Rashan didn't notice the smoke, didn't act like he'd heard me. I guess I should be used to that by now, but it was a lot like having a missing tooth. You were never aware of the tooth until there was this gaping hole in your mouth and you couldn't chew on that side.

I walked on silently, scuffing my green plastic jeweled flip flops in the sand. I must have scuffed a little too hard 'cause suddenly Rashan sneezed, that loud full-body sneeze that he had. I'd never known a black man with allergies before. Secretly I thought there was something unnatural about it. Something not right, like when a kid is labeled a genius but the combined IQs of both redneck parents don't equal the horsepower of their old Dodge truck. That kind of thing.

I kept flapping my flip-flops. Rashan didn't glare at me, just set his black enameled conga drum in the sand, removed a faded old red bandana from his pocket and daintily blew his nose. His long dread locks were tied back on his head, held tight by a matching bandana.

"Smoky," I tried again.

"Umm," he nodded in agreement this time. "Dusty," he pronounced, picked up the conga by the orange and green woven straps, turned to me to for help arranging the drum comfortably across his bare dark shoulders.

Rashan and I had met a week ago at a drumming circle in Gainesville. And now, here we were at Paralounge Drumming Festival at the Spirit of the Suwannee River Music Park. He had a tent and I had Sabrina, my old faded blue Mustang. Rashan was friends with one of the drummers in the African Conga group, Ashanti, who were performing later this afternoon. I could see how much he wanted to become part of their group.

"I'm hoping for my break here, woman." He refused to use my first name and simply called me "woman." He sneezed again, lighter this time, ran his arm under his nose and kept walking.

We showed our orange armbands to the two women at the welcome stand and they waved us through. I wondered if they paid us any notice. Even now I felt a certain edginess at being the red-headed half of a mixed race couple. Colorful beaded hair twists were woven through my hair, sparkling in the bright sunlight. I rotated my hips side to side in that sultry way I'd learned in belly dancing. The small bells dangling from the silver chain I wore around my hips jingled softly as I walked.

It was my dancing that drew Rashan to me last week. He drummed, I danced in the circle with the other women. The deep rhythmic tones from his drum caressed my body, rooted my feet to the ground in front of him. I whirled and gyrated as if I were Salomé dancing for King Solomon.

When at last the drumming stopped, Rashan walked right up to me, tilted my sweating head with his long dark fingers still hot from drumming, and in a heavy Jamacian accent whispered in my ear. "Woman, onct ya have black, ya never go back." He winked. And then he smiled that smile of his, strong white teeth, a striking contrast to the ebony sheen of his skin.

Mesmerized by his eyes, dark and mysterious, I thought if I touched him now, I would sink though Mother Earth clear to China.

Then he whispered in my other ear, caressed my cheek with a long dark index finger. "Ya my woman now. Don't leave me alone."

I've been his woman for seven nights now. I wondered what this circle would bring.

The drums sounded, Rashan's steps lengthened, I stirred up more dust in my haste to keep up. I knew he would speak no more to me until the circle broke up just before dawn.

"Black man don't talk to woman while he drumming. Bad mojo. Woman take energy that man need to drum. No speak, woman. Dance. No speak."

I admired the shape of his firm high butt as I followed him up to the small wooden stage.

Woman dance. No speak. When the dawn comes, the drums will be silent and the language we speak will need no words.

WHAT IF...

What if the Angel of Death came up to you
while you were walking down the road,
put her arm around your shoulders,
said I've missed you so,
and you were gone?

Remembering Nicole C

JESUS'S BIRTHDAY

I'm not celebrating Jesus's birthday this year.

He dropped by the other day when I was at my computer. He'll do that, you know, if you let Him "Do you have a minute?" He asked.

"Of course, I do, Lord, I always have a minute for you."

"Well, good, 'cause I need to talk and I want you to Google."

"Of course, Lord...."

"And stop calling me Lord, I'm tired of all that. Call me Jesus, or even Hey-sus, like the Hispanics. In my younger days, I was Little Joe, after my father, the man who raised me.

"No more Lord, this, Lord that, Son of God this, Savior of Man that."

Who could resist that look of his. But I could tell He was feeling down. He sounded tired, lonely. I wondered what could be troubling Him.

"That's what I want to talk about," He said before I could express my thought aloud. "Let's talk about how *you'd* feel if *you'd* come to earth billed as the Son of God, Savior of Mankind. Instead of being a blessing, you're now a great blemish leaving a legacy that caused the deaths of hundreds of millions of people.

101

"That's what I want you to Google. I'd like to know what those statistics are. Just how many people have died because of me in the last two thousand plus years? It must be mind-boggling by now."

My fingers were on the mouse, searching Google to see what I could find for answers to His question.

"Do you mind if I sit down?" He asked. "I feel as though I have the weight of the world on my shoulders."

He was already seated in the leather recliner, feet up, by the time I nodded, "Of course."

I'd Googled, "How many people have been killed by Christians?" and found a long article answering that question.

"This is interesting. It's divided into events, but doesn't give a cumulative total." I began reading. "Ancient Pagans. Here's a good one. World famous female philosopher Hypatia of Alexandria was torn to pieces with glass fragments by a hysterical Christian mob led by a Christian minister named Peter, in a church, in 415."

I wasn't sure how world famous she was, I'd never heard of her, but that was pretty brutal.

"Go on." Jesus had His eyes closed, one arm draped across His forehead.

"Okay. Next is….the Crusades, they're always good. Pope Urban II, fought two different battles in Hungary. Killed thousands in each. Then conquered Jerusalem, July 15, 1099. Estimated sixty thousand killed."

Jesus rubbed his eyes. "Oh, I remember that one, all right. Keep going."

"Here's an estimate that from 1095 to 1291, over five million were killed in the Holy Crusades. Then it goes on. Heretics and Atheists, over a million. Some burned at the stake, some hanged, most killed in battles."

102

"Well, the numbers are climbing, but I think we've just started the wheel spinning." At least He'd opened His eyes and was looking at me.

Suddenly I remembered my manners. "May I offer you something to drink?"

"Some wine would be good. Would you like red?" Jesus smiled for the first time. "Seems appropriate, don't you think? The Blood of Christ?" An earthenware goblet appeared in His hand, a similar one on the coaster next to my keyboard. "Try it, I think you'll like it."

I sipped. It was delicious. I looked back at the screen. "There's more…"

"Read on, child, this is fascinating."

"Witches, several hundred thousand. Religious wars, and only a few are mentioned, millions. Then it goes on to Jews and Native Peoples. More millions."

I switched to a new site. "Here's one that lists all the murders mentioned in the Old Testament. Cumulative total, 2,391,421. Wow, and that's before it really started, isn't it?"

"That's what I'm saying. I wasn't even here yet and the killing was going on. Once I arrived, then met my unfortunate demise, it spun totally out of control. Even I can't stop it now." He took a big drink of wine. "So you're doing just what I'd like all of you to do, stop celebrating my birthday. It's not about me. It's never been about me. I wish people could see that it's about power, the absolute power that leads to absolute corruption."

I could tell He really needed to get this off His chest. I nodded and sipped as He spoke. I don't know how long we sat that way…a few minutes, several hours.

Eventually He rose from the recliner, thanked me for my patience and my listening ear, said, "Don't celebrate my birthday this year. It's more than I can bear. Embarrassing really, all this fuss and no one remembers the reason."

A hundred things to say flashed across my brain. I squinted my eyes and looked at Him closely. Oh, my gosh, He does have a halo. All those old Masters were correct in how they'd painted Him.

At this shock of recognition, I blinked…and He was gone. He'd taken His earthenware goblet of wine with Him. Mine was still sitting on the coaster next to the keyboard. I touched it, tightened my hold on the stem, and took another sip.

Then laughed.

That rascal. He'd turned that wonderful wine into water. The purest water I'd ever tasted.

COMMUNITY PLATE

Words engraved on the fork
resting in my hand.
A fork carefully designed,
forged into permanence.

Lines etched across the silver,
stretch into the past,
curve across the present,
endure into the future.

Rectangles crown the top,
bordered by triangles
holding in the form.
Tiny squiggles dance

a light spring breeze
in the craftsman's heart
that dark winter night as he works alone
in a building long since demolished.

Symmetry is in his heart,
the perfect symmetry of love, balance,
mystery, fortune, and family,
spacious enough to hold all that and more.

Susan Green Jaillet

His heart is full,
his thoughts still and silent
as he carefully constructs
the community so much a part of his world.

One that endures the years
serving, stabbing, resting, lying in a drawer
waiting for the next meal,
the next opportunity to shine and serve.

The hand that holds it,
in sickness, in anger,
as it flies across the table
nearly puncturing a face instead of a roast.

The stories in this Community Plate
lay hidden, dormant, until touched
by the one who can hear
the howl of the wind,

smell the oak burning low
in the cast iron stove
that warms his feet
that long ago night.

The one who can feel
the familiar touch of his
wife's lips
when at last he returns home

satisfied and tired,
to lie like a spoon
against the solid reality
of his beloved's back

on a cold winter night
so long ago.

CHURCH OF THE ETERNAL BAR-B-QUE

They begin on Friday night, before sunset. Summer, winter, fair skies or toad-drowning rain, I'd smell the wood smoke from the fire that burned all night. The aroma of sizzling pork, chicken, and an occasional goat often started drifting my way after midnight. By morning my stomach is growling, waking me early, saying *get up, get dressed, forget the coffee, go get some of those great smelling ribs, fresh collard greens, spicy cole slaw, a fat slice of buttered cornbread, and one large Styrofoam container of sweet tea, no ice.*

I lived next door to the Church of Jesus the Christ, Our Eternal Savior. The hand-painted sign next to the primitive unpainted wooden bar-b-que stand reads, "All Is Welcome!" Every Saturday morning the faithful were out there selling platters and sandwiches to local travelers until nothing remains. Sometimes it's eleven o'clock before that happens.

One cold blue morning I drove over to that delicious smelling bar-b-que. That morning I was the lucky person to get the last platter of the weekend.

Seated in a rickety lawn chair in front of the stand, halfway between the road and the rustic wooden shack, sat a woman. A large black woman who looked like she'd lost a winning million dollar lottery ticket at the juke joint last night, and boy was she pissed. Only her eyes moved—not even the thought of a smile—as she watched each step I took to get from the Mercedes to the counter. She was half in the chair, half out, halfway between the bar-b-que stand and the road. The human version of a surly pit bull on a short chain. Can't get neither here nor there and mad as hell at just having to show up.

The couple behind the counter said pleasant good mornings, how can we hep' yas, and I placed my order—whatever it was they still had some of. They were happy to see this last platter go. I tipped them three dollars and they offered to show me their new church, built with their bar-b-que proceeds. The older black woman smiled, showing a few remaining teeth, when I said yes. I wished I'd put down a five.

I followed the woman and her husband across the dirt drive, waited while he pulled open one of the heavy wooden doors, and ushered me in. The husband led me down the center aisle, caressing each polished pew as we passed. He muttered his name, but I didn't understand him, so I just smiled and followed, nodding my head, hoping I didn't look as uncomfortable as I felt.

"Built these myself, wi' wood from my cousin's mill in Georgia. Brung it down hisself, he did, a load a month for two years." He stopped, turned away from me, briefly covered his mouth with his hand, turned again to face me. He was an aging man, looked like he'd seen many a day of hard work but he was still moving, though a bit slowly. A kind man, he seemed. A survivor.

"New dentures," his wife looked at him. "The Medicaid paid for 'em. Don't seem to fit him right."

She was short and round, pleasant as a spring squash blossom, down to the bright yellow apron she wore.

She took my hand, led me forward. "Our baptismal font," she pointed to the tall, square structure near the pulpit, nearly as tall as I. Three wooden steps lead up to it. "Dunkin' is what we do. None of that sprinkling like some of 'em. Total immersion in the Lord, startin' here."

She smiled up at the wooden cross above the altar. "My son made that." She turned back to me. "Jest after he come home from Raiford, many long years ago. Finished it right 'fore he was killed."

"That cross is beautiful, you must be so proud," I said. I smiled, nodded, uh-hummed, but I didn't ask how her son had been killed.

The tour resumed. "Preacher says total immersion is what we need." I looked at the water bubbling in the tank. I'd seen smaller backyard pools.

She turned and started back down the center aisle, waited for me to catch up.

"Thank you for showing me your church."

Her husband closed the big door behind us. "We now does lock it," he mumbled. "The Lord protects those who do his work, but He does 'spect us to take care of His things."

He shook his head as he removed the key from the solid lock. Another turn of the head for denture adjusting, and he led the way to my waiting Styrofoam to-go box. "Bless you, now, bless you. Come join us any Sunday, you hear?"

I smiled, realizing I'd be as welcome here as in any church I'd ever enter.

"Thanks, I just might do that," I said, knowing all along I never would.

I walked to the car, risked another look at pit bull woman who did seem to be sitting just a bit straighter in that rickety lawn chair. She was still staring at my car, a 1979 Mercedes 500 SLC, painted metallic purple.

She waited until I pulled the handle on the driver's side door before she spoke. What she said still makes me smile.

"I likes yore ride," she drawled. And then she actually grinned, big white teeth in a round dark face.

Driving home, I inhaled the aroma of those ribs, collard greens and yellow corn bread with one slab of butter. I thanked the Church of Jesus the Christ, Our Eternal Savior.

I knew I would return next Saturday to my favorite roadside altar.

THE HEARTLAND

I'm from the Heartland.

I'm from the city Sandburg called hog butcher of the
world.

I'm from the rich, black, loamy soil along the 39th parallel,
the path of the transcontinental arc across America,
the line the last glacier left as it receded
as majestically and mysteriously as it appeared.

I'm from the neighborhoods where Italians lived
next to Poles in brick walkups,
their rich languages filled my ears.

I'm from the ground floor apartment next to the
holy-roller church where black voices sang and
praised so loud that my dad would
bang on the wall with a shoe and yell,
but they never stopped.

I'm from the steel and grease and
bearings of oil wells that toiled,
day and night, summer and winter,
pumping crude oil from the ground.

I'm from the blood of horse traders, bootleggers,
blacksmiths, ferrymen, and farmers.

I'm from the railroad, the countless miles of track
lubricated with the sweat and blood of everyone's
father, uncle, brother, grandfather
as it inched tie by tie across the plains.

I'm from the apron strings of mothers and grandmothers
who did what had to be done to survive
and keep their children alive.

I'm from the community of stoic, hardy souls
coming together once a year with their green beans,
their corn, their tomatoes, to simmer chowder
a day and a night in huge iron kettles
beneath the maple trees.

I'm from the Ball jars stored in my grandpa's garage,
dusty and unused for a season because the drought
had dried the soil and parched every living thing
trying to make a life in it.

I'm from the flat farm land that a hundred years earlier
didn't know whether its heart was Blue or Grey.

I'm from the Land of Lincoln where only Blue
was taught in our school's version of history.

I'm from the halls of Bennett School where
I learned there was so much more to the world
than what I had seen.

I'm from the gold and grey uniforms of our superior
Greenwave marching band and the chalk that marked
the grids across the high school football field.

I'm from the corn fields, golden tassels waving in the wind, and the beauty of crystalline rows of soybeans that left me dazed one hot summer day.

I'm from the Heartland.

ABOUT THE AUTHOR

Born in Chicago, Susan grew up downstate in Mattoon, Illinois. After graduating from Eastern Illinois University with a B.S. in Business and a M.S. in Education, she held several positions at Lake Land College in Mattoon.

In Florida she spent twenty-seven years in public education. Twenty five were at Lake Technical Center, first as the Displaced Homemaker/Single Parent Program Counselor, then teaching business and computer software applications. After retiring she wrote the Green Scene column and copyedited for Pulse the Magazine in Mount Dora. She has edited several books for local writers.

Susan is an active member of Writers One Flight Up and helps sponsor and judge writing contests and events in conjunction with the W.T. Bland Library. She is published in three anthologies. This is her first book of short stories and poetry. Her first novel, inspired by events occurring during her time with Lake County Schools, will be available in 2018.

Made in the USA
Lexington, KY
11 December 2017